Mastering the Problems of Living

Mastering the Problems of Living

By

HARIDAS CHAUDHURI

Professor of Integral Philosophy
and Psychology. President, California Institute of Asian Studies,
San Francisco, President, Cultural
Integration Fellowship.

Foreword by R. Gordon Agnew

Professor Emeritus, University of
California Medical Center, San Francisco

A QUEST BOOK

Published under a grant from the Kern Foundation

THE THEOSOPHICAL PUBLISHING HOUSE
Wheaton, Ill., U.S.A.
Madras, India / London, England

© Haridas Chaudhuri, 1968
First Quest Edition published by the Theosophical Publishing
House, Wheaton, Illinois, a department of The Theosophical
Society in America, 1975

Chaudhuri, Haridas.
 Mastering the problems of living.

 (A Quest book)
 Reprint of the ed. published by Citadel Press, New York.
 Includes bibliographical references.
 1. Life. 2. Conduct of life. I. Title,
[BD431.C467 1975]   128'.5   75-4172
ISBN 0-8356-0463-2

PRINTED IN THE UNITED STATES OF AMERICA

To Mahatma Gandhi

Foreword

BY DR. R. GORDON AGNEW

The sensitivity of the Oriental scholar has long held the respect and the attention of the Occidental world. The term "The Wisdom of the East" has not been lightly or casually applied to that great repository of thought and feeling which, over long centuries, has accumulated, in depth and in comprehensiveness. This invaluable resource is rightly available to the enquiring and searching mind of the reflective Westerner.

The pragmatic Occidental mind is schooled predominantly to the objective, the concrete, and the tangible, and is rather elated by the relative ease with which sequential discovery and unfolding of some of the problems and some of the hypotheses of the scientific world has been achieved. However, the Westerner is today most properly sobered by the increasing realization that his newer insights, impressive as they are, reveal threatening vistas of destructive sequelae which are synchronous with attractive vistas of material progress and material potentials of comfortable living. It should, therefore, not be a matter of surprise, today, to find

7

that many of our young men and women, in spite of the material abundance of their environment, are, in their searching, critical and prone to question our ethical, moral, and spiritual values. In the face of our rather well-fed complacency and our relative indifference to the humanitarian ideals and the authoritative patterns of our still nominally recognized Occidental religious and ethical systems, they are often confused and rebellious.

A treatise on the problems of existence requires no apologetic and no defensive *raison d'être*. I would find it hard to conceive of an individual of intelligence and sensitivity who would not consciously and subconsciously respond to such a theme, and who would not recognize, within himself, a need, and perhaps an urgent need, for the consideration of such vital problems as are discussed within this book. Its chapters encompass profound contemplation of inescapably significant aspects of living—as an individual seeking self-fulfillment and seeking oneness with all of Nature and with Being, and as an integrated member of the human community on a local, national, and international level —in terms of creative communication and creative functioning.

On our campuses, in our discussion groups, and wherever meaningful dialogue enlivens and enriches human relationships one is likely to hear, with new emphasis, reference to the essential nature of the study of human ecology—of the effort of man to understand his environment and to recognize his widening role in the creative implementation of his relationship to it.

To interpret and to articulate the problems of existence, in terms of human ecology, it is a fortunate coincidence that Professor Chaudhuri is able to bring to his

deliberations the insights of both the East and the West.
It will be an immeasurable advantage to the student of
human problems to have available, in the systematic
appraisal and evaluation of the intellectual and emotional factors involved, the guidance of this distin-
guished scholar. In India, he is a recognized authority,
as teacher and as writer, on the philosophies of Asia.
Learned in the accumulated wisdom of long centuries,
he is friend and associate of many outstanding philosophers, poets, and artists of that country. However, the
qualifications of the author are not delimited by his
eminent Eastern background. In the spirit of the true
student he has also explored the substantial dimensions
of Occidental philosophy, psychology, and sociology.
With rare perception and observation he has offered, in
his lectures and in his writings, clarifying consideration
of basic convergences of concept and significant dissimi-
larities of thought and feeling between the Orient and
the Occident.

Doctor Chaudhuri's "laboratory" has been an effective aid to his understanding of American life and an
invaluable vehicle for his service to the community. In
San Francisco he is Chairman of the Department of
South Asia in the American Academy of Asian Studies,
and he is President of the Cultural Integration Fellowship. The Fellowship Center, the "Ashram," is the focal
point at which Eastern and Western scholars and students meet—for fellowship, for the dialogue vital to true
communication, and for mutual search for higher
values.

We are indebted to Professor Chaudhuri for this
provocative and challenging work, and for this latest
evidence of his desire to share with us from the depth of
his mind and heart. He has, with frankness and vision,

discussed basic concerns, such as the question of human anxiety, depression, and despair; he has with clarity delineated the vital importance of decision-making, and the crucial need of wisdom in human relations. He has probed deeply into the inner life of the individual, into the role of meditation and the problem of identity. He has, without hesitancy, creatively considered the meaning of Death. Writing of the Self, he points out with candor that "among grievously erroneous notions of spirituality is the belief that a spiritual person must be selfless to the extent that he must have no independent view or a decision of his own"; and in a later section, he states, "It is in dynamic self-realization that the physical, emotional, intellectual and moral aspects of personality fall into their right places; each functions as instrumental to the creative self-expression of the authentic self as an active center of the eternal." In the final chapter the author, from his mature experience, offers an hypothesis on the ultimate theme of "How to Live a Balanced Life"; and in this arresting message the theoretical and the practical, the abstract and the concrete assume dimensions of enlightening value.

From ancient China a traditional aphorism, still known by everyone, runs "Si Hai Ti Hsiong"—that all men within the four seas may be brothers. This statement is by no means viewed as a platitude; its meaning is both practical and profound—it overrides ethnic, cultural, or temporal considerations and holds that men indeed may live, as individuals or as groups, in integrated understanding and fellowship. John Donne, in seventeenth-century England, left on the lips of men the imagery that "No man is an island, entire of itself . . . because I am involved in Mankind." The late philosopher Martin Buber portrayed interpersonal and intergroup relationships of such outgoing "I-Thou" authenticity that new creative communication is achieved. Haridas Chaudhuri, in this book, is vividly portraying the urge in the East and in the West toward the unremitting search for the maturation of the individual and the wholeness of human society.

Contents

Author's Preface ... 15

I The Problem of Existence ... 21

II How to Conquer Depression ... 36

III How to Overcome Anxiety ... 53

IV How to Rise Above Despair ... 71

V How to Make Decisions ... 84

VI The Problem of Suffering ... 101

VII Wisdom in Human Relations ... 119

VIII The Meaning of Death ... 140

IX Meditating for Self-Perfection ... 158

X The Problem of Identity ... 187

XI How to Live a Balanced Life ... 203

Author's Preface

The present volume is based upon lectures I have given, on numerous occasions over the years, at the East-West Research Center and under the auspices of Cultural Integration Fellowship, San Francisco.

These lectures were more in the form of a sustained dialogue than an exposition of set views. I saw the crisis of our age reflected in the anxious inquiries of young people attending our classes and meetings. I felt the pulse of those desperately searching for life's meaning beyond mere platitudes and high-sounding verbiage. What good are ethical injunctions and religious sermons if they are unrelated to the fundamental problems of life in a given historical situation? What good are fanciful philosophical theories if they afford no help in grappling with the problems of existence which confront man in his most crucial moments?

Divorced from the context of actual existence, ethics, religion, and philosophy do indeed lose all meaning. They become so many avenues of escape from reality. They help people bypass the burning issues of life and settle down with smug complacency in a subjective realm of wishful thinking. But with an existential orientation, ethics, religion, and philosophy have each a vital role to play in man's self-development. Each elucidates an essential aspect of human personality, and throws light upon a particular area of life. They are all indispensable in the integral development and complete fulfillment of one's being.

Discussed in this book are such basic problems of existence as egocentricity and immaturity, anxiety and identity, depression and despair, suffering and death, human relations and decision-making, self-estrangement and one-sidedness. Reference has frequently been made to the findings of modern psychology in throwing light upon the roots of these problems in the human mind. But mere psychological insight is not enough for an effective solution of life's problems.

Human reality is multidimensional in character. Man is not just a self-enclosed psycho-physical entity. He has also the social, religious, and ontological aspects of his being. The psychical, the socio-ethical, the religious, and the ontological are inseparably interwoven in the complex structure of his existence. As a social being, he cannot find happiness through mere preoccupation with his own individual pleasure. Concern for social welfare is a vital factor in his well-being. By virtue of his religious aspect, he cannot live without some faith. He needs an ideal for which he can live, and to preserve which he would be willing to die. It is through total commitment to a positive set of values that his life becomes meaningful. Finally, man has an ontological dimension. His social and interpersonal relations as well as his conception of purpose and value derive their meaning, in ultimate analysis, from his world-view. Who is man? What is his place in the universe? How is he related to the ultimate ground of all existence? What is the meaning of death? What light does it throw upon the purpose of life? Man's search for meaning and meaningful living, his search for happiness and fulfillment, cannot be complete without finding some kind of answers to these most fundamental of all questions.

The basic issues of existence are of such a nature that only an existential solution to them can be ultimately satisfactory. Each individual has to find the answer, each has to discover the truth afresh, in the depths of his own being, in the context of his own living experience, in the course of his own inner evolution. Each has indeed to work out his own salvation.

The discussion of this book is therefore necessarily in the nature of finger-pointing to the truth. It consists of clarification and elaboration of the problems that vitally concern us. It distinguishes, as briefly as possible, the psychological, ethical, religious, and ontological aspects of the problems. It suggests the lines along which the problems can be tackled with some hope and confidence. But all these, it must be remembered, are not intended as ready-made solutions—simply because there can be no ready-made solutions. They are intended to set the direction in which one may hopefully look for the solution. They are intended to offer help, by stimulating thought and by awakening the power of faith, to those who are searching for that light of truth which alone can save. How far the author has been successful in this effort the reader alone can judge.

My grateful thanks are due to Dr. R. Gordon Agnew for his kindly writing a Foreword for this book. His fervent dedication to the goals of human ecology has been to me a source of inspiration. Sincere thanks are also due to the Board of Directors, Cultural Integration

Fellowship, for their kind permission to incorporate in this volume my lectures given under its auspices. Finally, I should like to take this opportunity of thanking Edith Reames, Lucille Tarbell, and Gladys Nordquist for their devoted services in transcribing the tapes and preparing the typescript.

HARIDAS CHAUDHURI

San Francisco
August 1967

Mastering the Problems of Living

CHAPTER I

The Problem of Existence

THE PROBLEM OF EXISTENCE has come to the foreground of consciousness in our age. There are several reasons for this.

First of all, we have to reckon with the reality of the Atomic Age. We stand today at the crossroads of history. Mankind is faced with a crucial choice between atomic annihilation and peaceful co-existence. The menace of global destruction caused by a single mistake or false step made somewhere in international politics hangs over the head of modern man like the sword of Damocles.

Viewed against the backdrop of the last two great wars, the harnessing of atomic energy has enormously heightened the contingency of life, the precariousness of existence. Our life hangs indeed by a very thin thread. Anything may happen at any moment. Faith in the rationality of man has been shaken. Faith in the rationality of the world made secure by an all-good personal God has also been shaken. This loss of faith is only being confirmed every day by the bizarre happenings—senseless automobile accidents, urge killings, sex murders, suicides, and the like—reported by our daily newspapers. Mr. Jones, returning home from his office, is suddenly caught in a fatal accident caused by the mad rush of a daredevil driver—and so he never comes home. A young girl on her way home from school is treacherously kidnapped by a sexual pervert—and her parents never see her again. More than a hundred people, traveling in a first-class airplane, are mercilessly killed by the sudden explosion of a time bomb planted there by a madman. Where is then the security of life in today's much-vaunted civilization?

Industrial revolution has enormously enhanced our sense of insecurity by disrupting traditional family life and the peaceful village community. In big industrial centers human relations are largely dehumanized. They have become formal and impersonal, ruled by the concept of doing business. When everybody wants to do business with everybody else, nobody can reach the heart of anybody. So the heart goes out of business. And with the heart go out of sight all specifically human values. Consequently, those who have any heart left in them suffer. Witness the operation of Gresham's Law in the field of human relations. The heartless, the tough-minded ones, drive the tender-hearted out of circulation. Existence is threatened with a pervasive feeling of emptiness and nothingness. With all the luxurious things that money can buy, life loses its meaning.

Scientific revolution has snatched away from man his age-old emotional crutches. Traditional faith in the supernatural order as the origin and real home of man has been eroded. The time-honored illusions of personal immortality and a blessed hereafter have been shattered. The rosy expectations of heavenly rewards have been pricked like soap bubbles. His comfortable religious castle demolished, man stands exposed today to the cold piercing winds of chance and change, of hard work and fatal risk, of do-or-die prospects. In consequence, existence has assumed the frightening proportions of a crucial problem.

It is, however, not my intention here to go into the social, economical, political, and philosophical aspects of the problem of existence. I shall confine myself to a brief discussion of the issue from the psycho-spiritual standpoint.

In what different ways do people react to the problem of life? What are the different ideals of existing and attaining self-fulfillment? What is the most integrated ideal of existence?

Ancient sages compared life to a perpetual flow, to an ever-changing stream. To live successfully is to be able to cross the river of life. Those who fail to cross it ruin the potential of existence.

There is a nice old story about an unsophisticated boatman and a sophisticated scholar. The scholar got into a small boat and requested the boatman to take him across the river. Pretty soon, the scholar struck up a learned conversation. He chanted a few verses from Gītā and then asked the boatman, "Do you remember the eighteenth chapter of the Bhagavad Gītā?" The boatman said, "No sir, I don't." After a pause the scholar asked again ,"Have you read the Katha Upaniṣad?" The boatman hung his head in shame and said, "No sir, I have never been to any college or seat of higher learning." But still the scholar kept asking similar questions. When the boat was about in the middle of the stream there was lightning in the sky and rumblings of thunder could be heard. It seemed a storm was coming. It was now the turn of the boatman to ask the scholar a little question. "Do you know, sir, how to swim?" The scholar said, "No, I don't." "In that case how would you save your life if we are caught in a storm and the boat capsizes?"

The art of existence is the art of swimming in the stream of life. It is the ability to cross and recross the flux of time by boat if available, by swimming if necessary, and by both when the boat fails after going part of the distance.

Let us now consider, with the help of the analogy of the river, the different ways people react to the problem of existence.

IMMATURE ONES

Some people stand on the bank of the river with fear and trembling. As they look into the swift current of the river and its dark eddies, they feel frightened. As they look at the vague, shadowy, almost invisible, outline of the outer shore, fear of the unknown fills their minds. They can never muster courage to get into the river. They are the mentally immature ones. They are scared to death in the face of life's baffling problems. They feel paralyzed when faced with the rough-and-tumble of adult society. They secretly long, and long desperately, to go back into the father's affectionate arms or the mother's absolutely secure lap. They refuse to go forward. They wish to regress. Or, sitting on the bank of the river and looking heavenward, they may create in their minds a big cloud-cuckoo land of subjective fancy and choose to levitate freely therein.

IMPRACTICAL ONES

Some people have a strong desire to cross the river of life. But they never get to learn how to swim. They want to cross by riding on the shoulders of somebody else. They depend absolutely upon some hired hand. But in the event of the failure of external help they are doomed.

They are the excessively intellectual or one-sidedly emotional types of people. Like the vain scholar in the story above, they seek solution in scholarship and erudition. They consider book learning to be the equivalent of wisdom. They neglect to get acquainted with the ways of the world. Consequently, with all their good intentions they are naïve and impractical. They close their minds to the ever-new facts of experience, to the fresh developments of the surging stream. So every now and then they get submerged, if not completely drowned, in the currents and cross-currents of life.

The same is true of the excessively emotional type of people. Frequently carried off by waves of emotion, they lose their grip upon the stern realities of the actual world. Used to beholding things and events through the prism of emotion, they fail to see things as they are. Unsure of their own vision, they tend to lean too much on others. They get entangled in diverse bonds of emotional attachment. Convinced at heart that the problem of existence can be solved emotionally, they unconsciously drift into emotional fixation upon somebody big and strong. Thus they surrender their own ability to walk or to swim. The important thing to remember in this connection is that neither abstract intellectualism nor weak-kneed emotionalism is an answer to the problem of life. Both intellect and emotion must be pressed into the service of personality growth. They are aids to the development of one's own strong independent character. "To exist is to choose," as Jean-Paul Sartre says. One must develop this power of free choice or independent decision. In doing so, the development of intellectual ability to obtain objective and unprejudiced information about all relevant facts and viewpoints is necessary. Also necessary is the development of emotion so that one can be in warm rapport with fellow beings and co-workers. There can be no substitute for genuine love and sympathy. Love begets deep understanding and transforms it from cool calculation into warm-hearted participation. It transforms knowledge from vainglorious self-seeking into compassionate self-giving.

INDIVIDUALISTS

Then again, there are people who want to cross the river of life in a big hurry. With any means at their disposal, or by traveling any path open to them, they want to reach the other shore. And having reached the other shore, they are reluctant to come back. They wish to forget all about their origin, their connections with fellow beings, and the delights and dangers of their life on the river or on the land of birth.

They are the avowed individualists. They are mainly concerned with their private self-fulfillment or personal salvation. From the secular standpoint, they are the narcissistic type of people who are, all their life, wrapped up in the ego. They may have talent. They may make a big success through prodigious effort. But they do not care for others. "After me the deluge" is their motto. They want to see their own image deified and worshipped everywhere. They hate to undergo any suffering for the sake of a fellow being. By the inexorable law of Karma, usually they end up lonely and deserted. Their crown of success and glory may one day turn to ashes. Utterly crestfallen, one day they may have to cry in the wilderness.

Religiously speaking, they are the personal salvationists or world and life negating mystics. They are impetuously eager to cross the river of time and to contact the nontemporal or the supernatural. They live all their lives with gaze fixed upon the supernatural glory in the hereafter. Or, by ignoring the swift-moving current of evolution, they become absorbed in the contemplation of the unchanging and the eternal.

In the west they are ascetics and hermits. They are other-worldly, oriented to the supernatural. In the east, they are the world-renouncing *sādhus* and mystics. Indifferent to time and its movement toward the future, they are oriented to the eternal that transcends past, present, and future. In their intense concentration upon the eternal, they ignore both history and the beacon light of the future. They experience complete disintegration of their ego and mind. Their individuality is swallowed up in the vastness of the infinite. All their springs of action are dried up. All desire gone, they lose initiative and drive for action. So having reached the other shore they never come back.

COSMIC MEN

Then, there are people who, having reached the other shore, come back. However long they may be gone in their search for truth in solitude, on gaining illumination they return to society. They are eager to share their profound peace and illumination with their fellow beings on earth. They are not content with their own personal salvation, but dedicate themselves to the goal of cosmic liberation. In Christianity this goal is called the kingdom of heaven. In Mahāyāna Buddhism it is called *mahā karunā*, i.e., concern for the liberation of the whole creation. In Hinduism this is known as *sarva-mukti*, which means the liberation of all. So in the case of the above type of persons, personal salvation is not the final goal, but a means to a still higher goal, namely, collective liberation of the world. They are moved by the spirit of love and compassion.

Those who dedicate themselves to cosmic welfare may be called cosmic men. Broadly speaking, there are three types of cosmic men: other-worldly, this-worldly, and integral.

The other-worldly type of cosmic men look upon the phenomenal world as a mere appearance of the transcendent. They may be oriented to the supernatural kingdom of God, from the standpoint of which the natural order of existence seems utterly evil. Or, they may be oriented to that timeless reality from the standpoint of which this world of space, time, and evolution appears illusory or unreal. So even though they return to society after spiritual liberation, their chief mission is to assist their fellow beings to cross the stream of phenomenal existence over to the other shore.

It is immaterial for our purpose here whether the other shore is conceived of as the supernatural or as the purely nontemporal. The humanitarian services of other-worldly cosmic men are directed to the ultimate end of renouncing the natural world with a view to gaining the surpassing peace of the other shore. Thus while dedicating themselves to the cosmic welfare, they refuse to be integrated with the life of the cosmos. They feel themselves as descendents of Father Heaven, and so they disown Mother Earth. Or they feel themselves to be children of immortality to such an extent that they disown time, and disregard its call for historic action. They refuse to be children of earth or of time. In the midst of all their actions on earth their mind is elsewhere—out of this world.

The this-worldly or existential type of cosmic men are down-to-earth in their outlook. They stand at the opposite pole from the other-worldly type. They lay emphasis upon the world of space, time, and evolution as the one ultimate reality. For them Being is perpetual becoming. Human reality is history. To exist is to change, to grow, to become. The nontemporal has no ontological priority over the process of time. It is nothing but the sphere of human aspiration and ideal. The eternal is just the realm of values which have no reality apart from human consciousness and desire.

Karl Marx, Bertrand Russell, Jean-Paul Sartre, Albert Camus, and the like may be counted among this-worldly cosmic men. Their cosmicity lies in their sincere dedication to the total human welfare. Their emphasis is upon the betterment of the conditions of living for the masses of the people the world over. They are liberated, not in the traditional religious sense, but in the humanistic sense of the term. They are liberated from the narrow limitations of racism, parochialism, cultural provincialism, exclusive nationalism, etc.

The one flaw in the approach of the this-worldly type of cosmic men is their lack of appreciation of the nontemporal dimension of Being. In their justifiable protest against other-worldliness and supernaturalism, they swing back to the opposite extreme and turn a blind eye to the value and reality of the nontemporal as the foundation of all existence in time. It is a glimpse of the nontemporal in some form or other which has been at the source of much of the sublimest creation of man in art, literature, religion and philosophy. The spiritual potential of man is left unfulfilled without a discovery of the timeless ground of his existence. Alienated from the nontemporal dimension of Being, he is indeed condemned to be "a futile passion." All his affluence in terms of material possessions is likely to appear empty and shallow. It may be difficult—yes, extremely difficult—to define the essential structure of the eternal. But however difficult to define, the eternal is inextricably entwined in the structure of human reality.

INTEGRAL COSMIC MEN

Finally, let us consider the integral type of cosmic men. Integral cosmic men are true to the kindred points of heaven and earth. They are true to both time and eternity. For them the eternal is not only the realm of ideas and values. It is the ultimate foundation of both things and ideas, of facts and values, of existents and essences. It is also the ultimate ground of all becoming, of creative as well as destructive processes, of evolution as well as dissolution.

Having seen the light of heaven, integral cosmic men do not disown Mother Earth, nor do they cease to be children of earth. They seek to transform themselves—their whole being—by that heavenly light. They consider both shores of the stream of time to be real. On the other side of the stream is the glory of pure transcendence, the eternal, the supra-cosmic Divine. On this side of the stream is Nature evolving, civilization unfolding, man creatively expressing himself in ever-new forms and values.

So the integral type of cosmic men, on return to society after their vision of the eternal, not only dedicate themselves to the cosmic welfare. They resolve to bring heaven upon earth. They resolve to bring something of the light of the eternal, something of the perfume of the infinite, into the flux of human affairs and social relations. They wish to build a new world order in the light of the splendors they beheld on the other shore. They wish to participate in the evolutionary being of this world, here and now, as a channel of expression of the eternal. They are not only dedicated to cosmic good but also integrated with cosmic life. They have no feeling of estrangement either from earth or from heaven, either from society or from eternity. United with the eternal through spiritual enlightenment, they are also united with the creative force of evolution, or with the spirit of history, through existential concern and participation. As Martin Heidegger says, it is in the "belonging together of man and Being"* in a common concern that the highest fulfillment of life lies.

The integral cosmic man is a man of integral truth consciousness. He is not only a *Bodhisattva* but a *Vijñānasattva*. He has not only deep concern for cosmic welfare. He aims at the transformation of the cosmic order into an image of the Supreme Being, into a unified world order of peace, love, justice and freedom. His enlightenment not only penetrates to the mystery of the eternal. It also embraces the profound significance of time, evolution, and history.

CONCEPT OF RENUNCIATION

There are some who think that in order to be able to participate in the creative life of the eternal, intimate human relations must be renounced. They consider the emotional bonds of human love a positive hindrance

* Martin Heidegger, *Essays in Metaphysics*, Kurt F. Leidecker, trans. (New York: Philosophical Library, 1960), pp. 22-24.

to the spiritual task of bringing the light of the eternal into the life of earth.

The above attitude is well illustrated in the life of Søren Kierkegaard. He fell in love with Regina and was engaged to her. But within a year he had to break the engagement in order to approach God with the fullness of love. Somehow he felt his sweetheart Regina to be God's competitor. She appeared to stand in the way. He saw no way of accepting Regina into the scheme of his longing for God.

In adopting the above attitude, Kierkegaard, with all his existential concern, followed the medieval path of life-negation. As Martin Buber has rightly observed, Reginas have been created by God not to hinder but to help in the search for God. The policy of life-negation is like cutting the Gordian knot of spirituality instead of trying to untie it. To renounce is easy. It evades responsibility and exposure to life's hazards and hardships. To be able to accept the bonds and responsibilities of human love is a mark of courage and maturity. It requires self-confidence and an assurance of inner strength. It requires that mature faith in God which can turn all negativities into positive assets in life's creative adventure.

Given a self-confident attitude toward life, intimate human relations become a positive factor in the perfect realization of God. It is through the right kind of love-relationship between I and Thou that the eternal Thou, the voice of the Supreme, emerges as the unfailing companion, as the friend, philosopher and guide, of the human soul. The path of life-negation leads, at best, to a very one-sided contact with the Divine. It is the balanced affirmation of life in all its aspects that brings God closest to the heart as the ultimate meaning of life. It is through intelligent and comprehensive self-organization that God is realized as the Self of self. It is by assuming one's existential role in the drama of life that one can be fully united with God as the ground of existence.

SYMBOL OF PERFECT EXISTENCE

In Hindu philosophy there is a beautiful symbol for the perfect man, for the thoroughly integrated person. It is the image of the swan. There are many ideas enclosed in this image.

First, the swan is perfectly at home in all the elements of Nature. He can walk on land, swim in water, and also fly in the air. So a perfectly integrated individual is called a swan (*Hamsa*) because of his intelligent adjustment in all the spheres of existence. He is psychically integrated and so united with his own authentic self. The different elements of his personality, his various impulses, desires, aspirations, thoughts, feelings, and so on, are harmonized into a symphony of joyful self-expression.

Secondly, he is perfectly at home in the social environment. At peace with himself, he is also at peace with the outside world. Wherever he goes, in whatever part of the globe circumstances may place him, he feels himself to be among his kith and kin. However lofty his personal achievement, no vain conceit separates him from his fellow beings. Barriers of race, creed, and nationality melt in the warmth of his all-embracing heart. His understanding of the ways of the world and his profound sympathy with human suffering render him a source of spiritual comfort to all those who contact him.

Thirdly, he is integrated with the Supreme Being, the

eternal. United with the ultimate ground of existence, he attains the peace that passeth understanding. His whole being is filled with the light of wisdom and the spirit of love. He radiates light, love, and peace in invisible ways. His entire being vibrates with the joy of the eternal. And that joy contains healing power for those who are sick of mind and body and soul. From the perspective of the eternal, he beholds the dynamic and meaningful interrelationship of the other two spheres of existence, namely, self and society, spirit and nature.

Another implication of the swan symbol is supreme wisdom. The swan is all white, and whiteness is the color symbol of wisdom. Wisdom is the perfect awareness of reality in its multiform fullness. It is the awareness of the eternal as the ground of existence. It is the awareness of the self as the dynamic focus of the eternal. It is the awareness of the world as the kaleidoscopic field of manifestation of the eternal.

Still another implication of the swan symbol is spiritual discernment. It is believed, especially with regard to a particular type of swan, that he has the miraculous ability to separate milk from water for his own nourishment. So the human swan is the discerning soul who has a deep sense of values. He has the power of sharp discrimination between truth and falsehood, between beauty and ugliness. He can promptly separate things of universal significance and permanent value from things of local significance and transient value. He can distinguish with unerring insight between things that belong to God and things that belong to Caesar, and between values that center around the true self and those that stem from the not-self or the pseudo-self. His actions are guided by this unerring value-distinction.

Finally, the swan symbol implies creative harmony

and balance. It implies the dynamic interplay of the inner and the outer, of introversion and extroversion, of meditation and action. The Sanskrit word *Hamsa* for swan has two parts: *Ham* and *Sa*. *Sa* means He, the Supreme Being. It is the sound of exhalation, an act of going out and self-giving to the infinite. *Ham* means I, the self. It is the sound of inhalation, of turning inward in search of one's inmost center of being. On the physical plane, by means of rhythmical inhaling and exhaling an individual is in dynamic contact with the universal life force. He draws upon it and also gives out to it. On the spiritual plane also the same law of give and take, the law of self-finding and self-giving, takes place. A person who has realized the full potential of existence holds in balance the introverted and the extroverted tendencies of his nature. Meditation and selfless action are like the inhaling and the exhaling, the systole and the diastole, of his spiritual life. By means of meditation he is in active communion with his authentic self. He affirms himself as a unique focus of the eternal. By means of selfless action, he is in active communion with the outside world. He gives himself in the service of all. Such self-giving deepens his self-discovery. And self-discovery enriches his self-giving.

Thus existence reaches its height of glory in communion with the multidimensional Being.

CHAPTER II

How to Conquer Depression

DEPRESSION IS a widespread emotional problem. It is more common in its incidence than the common cold. And certainly it is more crippling and dangerous. Nine out of ten people suffer from it occasionally. Thousands of people are committed to hospitals for pathological depression. About twenty thousand or more Americans commit suicide every year in helpless submission to the dark whispers of deep depression.

Depression may be normal or pathological. Even the most normal people experience depression once in a while. But healthy individuals have natural resources to overcome it. The vital urge is irrepressible. The stream of life can submerge or surmount all obstacles in its way even though it may be temporarily blocked. The spirit in man refuses to be depressed too long by pressures and problems, by conflicts and crises. An insight into the various causes of depression can strongly fortify and reinforce the life impulse.

When depression assumes a pathological form, external help in the form of psychiatric treatment, hospital care, competent spiritual ministration, or the like becomes necessary. The situation, then, gets out of control for the depressed individual. The natural buoyancy and optimism of the life spirit is then shattered. But with proper training and education, an individual can be fortified and fore-armed against such a contingency. A sound understanding of the etiology of depression and a well-balanced philosophy of life can be man's best protection against the crippling or paralyzing effect of depression. Such spiritual weapons can also be immensely helpful in gaining a quick and complete recovery from psychopathic depression.

We shall briefly investigate here some of the main causes of depression. Once the causes are clearly known, remedies will suggest themselves. With reference to the various causes, the ways and means of conquering the problem of depression will be indicated.

FAILURE AT SCHOOL

Failure, frustration, or disappointment in life is a common cause of depression.

Young people sometimes sink into depression when they make poor grades or meet with failure in school or college. There are even cases of students committing suicide on account of their poor showing in an examination. It is good to remember that failures are an integral part of life. Life is compounded of failures and successes. There are many geniuses in the world whose early school records are rather poor. When a person has a strong determination or the right attitude toward life, failures can be stepping stones to success. In fact, we learn more from failures than from successes. After the initial shock of failure is absorbed, a person emerges stronger and wiser. He is better equipped to accomplish the goal of life by reason of a better understanding of his own points of strength and weakness, and also of a more realistic grasp of the difficulties and opportunities inherent in a given situation.

Failure in school is sometimes too depressing to students because exaggerated importance is attached to the results of school examinations. The attitude of the family or of persons in authority may cause strong feelings of shame and distress to be associated with scholastic failure. But it is good to remember that school results are not the final index to one's intelligence and latent possibilities. A student who fails in one group of studies may shine in another. One who fails in scholastic pursuits may shine in business enterprise or creative action. There is always the question of the hidden talents of the individual. There is the need for judicious selection of one's individual lines of self-development.

DISAPPOINTMENT IN LOVE

Disappointment in love or home life is a potent cause of depression. Let us imagine a young man deeply in love with his girl friend. He feels that he cannot live without her. And then one day he discovers that she has given herself to another person whom she is soon to marry. The shock of disappointment may be so unbearable that the young lover may withdraw into terrific depression. He may see darkness all around and reject life and society. He may seek a way out by committing suicide.

Similarly, a housewife who is very faithful and devoted to her husband may one day discover that he does not care for her so much any more. He is perhaps going around with another woman. Or he is perhaps so much intoxicated with success in business or politics that he has little time left for wife and children. So the gloom of despondency envelops her life.

If an individual is fore-armed with right knowledge about life, depression resulting from disappointment in love may prove only a passing cloud. Otherwise it may ruin one's life. Love should never assume the form of total attachment. It should not be equated with clinging. It should never be allowed to exceed the bounds of self-poise or to hinder the growth of self-existence. In one's love-life one should never come to the point of feeling that life is worthless without a particular love object. No particular person has that much absolute value. The act of investing the particular with absolute value is of the essence of blind attachment. It amounts to idolatry. True love affirms the particular love object only as a mode of manifestation of the absolute, not as the absolute. Consequently removal of one particular love object naturally causes sorrow, but should not diminish or destroy life. Absolute love is due only to the absolute. But since the absolute is no external object, since it is the ground of all existence, all particular objects of love can only serve as symbols of the absolute. They are factors in the full growth of love. They are meant ultimately to direct our love toward union with the absolute.

In our love-life our expectations are sometimes too extravagant. Reality is not tailored to fit such extravagant expectations. Consequently too many love relations terminate in tragic disappointments. It is good to remember that nothing human, nothing ephemeral, nothing of this earth, can completely satisfy the love requirements of the human soul. God alone can. Increasing appreciation of higher spiritual values is essential for deeper emotional satisfaction. As we shower love on a particular object or person, let us remember that such an investment should not become a rigid fixation. The channel of communication with the absolute or God should always be left open. If that can be accomplished, we cease to be too demanding or exacting in our love relations. We can even afford to love without expectation of reward or return. In that way love becomes more and more mature and spiritual. It becomes a free and spontaneous outflow of the joy that characterizes the soul attuned to the divine. It becomes an unconditional self-giving of the emotionally mature self.

In order to prevent emotional fixation, it is always desirable to have a diversity of interests in life. It is good to have many friends in life even when one is utterly faithful in conjugal love to one's partner. Besides the delight of family life, it is desirable to have some interest in social or humanitarian values. It is good to have some interest in cultural pursuits or spiritual inquiry. Diversified interest in manifold values sustains the free flow of love's energy. It prevents emotional rigidity and petrifaction. In consequence, disappointments and frustrations can easily be absorbed. Love can always be redirected afresh to well-chosen values. All particular objects of love must be understood, in ultimate analysis, as various modes of manifestation of the absolute, which is the pole-star of all emotional yearning. In the final analysis, it is the absolute which is loved in all finite things. In its passion for love, the soul is ultimately oriented to the absolute. A clear understanding of these fundamental spiritual truths is the final guarantee against all depression. When this truth is forgotten, man, in his longing for love, is subjected to a state of futile passion, as Jean-Paul Sartre says. But when we learn to remember and practice this truth, love begins to glow with the rich promise of glorious fulfillment.

There was a woman who was very home-loving and utterly devoted to her husband. She had very few close friends and she went out very little. She was resentful of her husband's excessive preoccupation with business affairs. But his first love was success in business. His volume of business was gradually increasing and his social circle was widening; he had less and less time to spend in his home. The wife was getting convinced that her husband did not love her any more. She became extremely sad and listless. She had a strong urge to take her life. One night her husband came home to see that she made an unsuccessful attempt at suicide. She was taken to the hospital. After a few months of treatment in the hospital, she came back home, apparently recovered. She seemed to be quite cheerful again. One morning she prepared breakfast for her husband and sent him to the office. She cleaned the house thoroughly and put everything in perfect order. Then she went to the barn and hanged herself.

This case shows that a person may be outwardly cheerful and yet inwardly depressed—and thus many emotionally disturbed people are prematurely discharged from hospitals, their cheerful appearance proving tragically deceptive. Behind the misleading mask of gaiety, one may be deliberately planning for self-destruction.

It is desirable for a person to have outside social interests, broad cultural and religious interests, besides his domestic life. It is also necessary to understand that a man cannot and should not be tied down too much within the confines of the family circle. That is quite contrary to the masculine makeup. The wife's possessiveness may drive the husband further and further away. When the wife gives up her possessiveness, she may possess much better. When the wife functions as a wife without any binding noose or tyrannical rod in her hand, her unobtrusive devotion can throw a natural bridge between home life and the expanding business life of the husband. On the husband's side it is desirable to understand that no amount of success in business, no amount of popularity at parties and clubs, can be a substitute for the simple delights of home life. If it is the wife's folly to try to cut down the husband's world to the size of the family, it is the husband's folly to cut out the wife's world from his life. In his decision to do so, he acts like a man who wants a tree to grow higher by uprooting it from the soil. Both man and woman have their roots in family life. In order to grow higher, they have also to strike their roots deeper in the love soil of the family. It is on the strong and stable foundation of roots deeply set in love, that the glory of happy self-fulfillment in social success can be achieved.

EMOTIONAL FLUCTUATIONS

Depression is often the periodic suffering of a certain moody type of personality. There are some people who go through strange emotional fluctuations or changing moods. Sometimes they see themselves on top of the world. They are elated and exuberant, ready to accomplish anything. They feel light and joyous like a balloon, freely soaring in the sky. But this mood of expansion and exultation is followed by the opposite mood of contraction and depression. Such changes may take place in the course of the same day or week, or they may occur at longer intervals. When in the mood of depression, a person feels that he is good for nothing; life holds

no charm or color for him. He loses all self-confidence
and suffers from guilt and inferiority. He feels like a flat
tire or a burst balloon. He begins to entertain death
wishes or nihilistic delusions. And this nightmarish
mood appears like a pitch dark night that is never going
to end.

When the emotional fluctuations of a moody personality assume unmanageable proportions, he is known in
psychiatry as a manic-depressive case. A pathological
case of this nature has to be cared for in a hospital and
be given competent psychiatric treatment. But adequate
psychological and spiritual understanding can enable a
moody person to improve his condition and prevent the
pathological turn of his emotional instability. The more
the causes of the emotional see-saw are known, the better equipped a person is to overcome it.

Up to a certain point it is natural and quite normal to
have an ebb and flow in one's affairs or in the stream of
one's available energy. But extreme reactions to such
ebb and flow create an emotional problem. There are
periods in the life of a person when the outlook of life is
bright, the joy of living is spontaneous, the will to accomplish is indomitable. Also everything appears to go
one's way and fortune smiles with exceeding kindness. It
is wise to make maximum use of such a favorable wind
as it blows. But some people react to it in an exaggerated way. They become overconfident and over-
estimate themselves. They turn a blind eye to their own
shortcomings and to the forces of darkness in the world.
They underestimate enemies and take friends for
granted. In the flush of enthusiasm and seeming success,
they may overexert themselves and become intemperate
in eating, drinking, and other habits. They feel strong
enough to act in utter disregard of the feelings and in-

terests of other people. In consequence the tables are soon turned as a strong reaction sets in. Excesses committed and overexertions made, provoke the opposite extreme of hopeless exhaustion, dull despondency. The ebb period is then magnified beyond proportions as interminable gloom and self-annihilation. Deep clouds darken the mental horizon, and they seem to have no silver lining. All the positive features of life are blacked out. One enters, as it were, into the terrible dungeon of self-punishment.

But excess on the negative side provokes, again, its opposite on the positive side. Extreme self-suppression turns beyond a certain point into exaggerated self-expansion and exaltation. Life force is like a strong, elastic string which cannot be suppressed forever. The irrepressible urges of life react against morbid contraction with an excessive rebound. Moreover the period of depression is, for some people, a term of punishment for the ego for its excesses during the buoyant mood. After serving its term of incarceration, the ego again feels justified in asserting itself beyond all bounds. But excessive self-indulgence sows the seeds of guilt feelings and repentance which, in due time, bring on the dark night of depression again. And thus it goes. It is like the story of the man who was involved in the vicious circle of whiskey and onions. After a bottle of whiskey he used to kill the smell of liquor by eating onions. But then he would proceed to kill the odor of onions, which he strongly disliked, by drinking whiskey again.

It is good to remember that like night and day, flow and ebb, spring and winter, there is the dynamic flow of opposites in our subjective existence also. An understanding of this law of psychical change would help reduce much psychic tension. A depressed person has a tendency to feel that his dark night will never end. Such a feeling worsens the situation. As soon as he remembers that even the darkest night passes away with the advent of dawn, and that even the blackest clouds may have a silver lining, the situation immediately improves. When a person hits bottom, he may remember that he cannot go any lower. Falling to the bottom actually may help one conquer the fear of hitting the bottom. The next movement can only be upward. Our emotional mood largely determines our line of thinking. In a gloomy mind we only perceive the gloomy facts of our life situation. We tend to ignore the silver lining even though it is there. Similarly in an exultant mood we tend to ignore the dark forces operative in life. It is desirable to practice restraint during the up phase of emotional mood. Similarly it is needful to keep alive the flame of faith and self-confidence during the down phase. Even when we are reduced to a helpless position, we can turn to the fountain source of all help and strength. It is always possible for man to draw upon the higher power of the Supreme that surrounds him. The collapse of the ego with all its resources may, with the right attitude, open new hidden springs of resourcefulness. Man's calamity can indeed become God's opportunity. Self-opening to the infinite can turn a curse into a blessing.

THE PRESSURE OF PERFECTIONISM

Some people fall into occasional spells of depression on account of their perfectionistic tendency. They set before themselves too lofty an ideal of virtue. They may be animated by the ideal of angelic purity or God-like holiness. They want to disown the animal side of human existence. They desperately fight to suppress such natural impulses of life as the longing for good food, comfort, loving companionship, personal distinction, social recognition, and so on. In following certain ideals, much energy is wasted just in keeping down the so-called lower impulses which can hardly be completely liquidated. A yawning chasm is created between the human actuality and the fancied ideal of a God-like perfection. Perception of this chasm throws a person into dizziness and depression. The inner psychical tension, the gulf between the actual and the exalted ideal, the concomitant guilt feeling, the colossal waste of energy entailed in an unending, internal strife—all these combine to produce depression in many pious, puritanical, and holy people. Depression releases self-destructive fury. Consequently lofty idealists and perfectionists often suffer from terrible anguish of the soul. They tread the path of slow suicide resulting often in premature death. Popular belief explains it as the price of goodness, or as a short-cut to heaven. But goodness does not have to pay such a tragic price. Nor should it be equated with a premature departure for heaven. It is good to remember that holiness in its essence is not self-mutilation but the wholeness of personality. Goodness in its essence is not the armed rebellion of the spirit against the flesh, but rather the happy union of the spirit and the flesh in the service of God.

Sometimes people go into depression because of imaginary failures. When they set too lofty goals—goals out of proportion to their abilities—even solid achievements appear as failures. A healthy, optimistic attitude turns failure into success. An unhealthy, unrealistic, perfectionistic attitude turns success into failure. It is part of wisdom to learn to accept and enjoy success without going overboard.

THE DIZZINESS OF SUCCESS

There are some people who go into depression at the height of their towering success and glory. It is common experience that such people appear incapable of enduring happiness. Let us take the case of a young man who, by dint of his hard labor and perseverance, was steadily rising to eminence in his career. The time came when his efficiency was recognized by higher authorities. He was given a big promotion with an enormous increase in salary. He was placed in charge of a separate establishment. For some time everything went fine. But suddenly one day something seemed to break. He lost his pep. Life began to look dark, very dark, without meaning or color. People around him seemed to form a dark conspiracy against him. The suggestion of poisoning seemed to be in the air at the places where he ate and drank. He felt like killing himself, like jumping in front of a train.

Several causes may combine to create a condition of this kind. Some people work hard and well so long as they can take orders from some superior authority. But they instinctively recoil from a situation where they have to assume responsibility and make decisions of their own. Pitchforked to a position of independent authority, they get dizzy and tormented with imaginary fears. Unfortunate childhood experiences undermine their self-confidence in situations of unrestricted freedom. It is submission to authority which is associated in their minds with goodness and virtue.

Some people cannot endure happiness and prosperity because deeply ingrained in their mind is the notion of crime. Virtue is unconsciously associated in their minds with hard struggle and suffering. Happiness is felt as the negation of virtue. Inner guilt feelings may also prompt one to think that one does not deserve happiness. To others, it is personal ambition which is a sin, so that the situation of success, glory, and social recognition is inwardly felt as some sort of devil's trap. Such notions are evidently the result of faulty ethics and religious teachings. As we become aware of them, many hidden causes of depression are removed. Life is compounded of success and failure, of unfavorable and favorable circumstances, of adversity and prosperity, opposition and recognition, frustration and fulfillment. It is important to be able to accept failure and frustration constructively, without losing heart. It is also important to be able to accept success and glory with thankfulness and joy without going overboard. It is needful to maintain, in all circumstances, favorable or unfavorable, the attitude of constructive living, in a spirit of dedication to life's higher values.

THE DEPRESSION OF MIDDLE AGE

Depression hits many people in their middle age. For women, the forties, and for men, the fifties, are a very critical period. This is the time when some radical changes take place in the endocrine gland system. People become aware of their diminishing physical power and of reduced opportunity for winning love. Some people react to these symptoms of the aging process with panic and depression. In acute form such depression is known in psychiatry as involutional melancholia.

Middle age is also the time when people begin to be concerned in a greater or lesser measure with the hereafter. The problem of death and the mystery of the beyond begin every now and then to haunt the mind. In consequence religious needs and philosophical impulses begin to be awakened. If there is nothing but confusion in the mind about these ultimate issues, depression may open its abysmal depths.

Another potent cause of middle age depression is the absence of a balanced ideal of life. People who have been extremely hedonistic or epicurean in their style of living become panicky in middle age. As soon as they feel that their youth is slipping and that the ability to enjoy life has declined, they experience the terror of death. Life loses its meaning. Then again, people who have been too self-effacing and socially oriented in youth suddenly wake up one day in old age to experience their diminished social usefulness. Children perhaps don't need them so much any more. New jobs don't come to them any more. New generations do not covet their company much. They are not flexible enough to make new social adjustments. They cannot keep pace any more with ever-changing patterns in the fields of fashion and in the realm of ideas. Every now and then they are reminded that they are old-fashioned, out of tune with the times. As soon as they are relegated to the back seat by society, they begin to experience disillusionment. There is no nucleus of self-sufficiency on which they can fall back. It is also likely that at this time they experience a new upsurge of self-interest and egoistic motive. Those who are brought up to look upon the urge of self-interest as an evil, become emotionally upset on discovering within them something of the devil of an ego. In consequence, they sink into depression with strong feelings of self-condemnation.

It is good to remember that age is a characteristic more of the body than of the spirit. A person is as young as he feels. Perpetual freshness is an essential characteristic of the spirit. With proper spiritual training a person can develop qualities of mental mobility and flexibility, and maintain them all his life. Flexibility is youth and freedom. The strength that is born of flexibility can overcome the disadvantage of declining physical powers. By keeping abreast of the latest developments in hygiene, dietetics, and medical science, one can also arrest the degenerative process considerably. One can form new habits conducive to prolonged health and longevity.

As has been seen, depression is often the result of a one-sided and unbalanced life plan. Pleasure, joy, happiness—these are an essential component of life. The joy of living is a sign of health. It is therefore foolish to associate evil with such innocent pleasures of life as good food, comfort, conjugal love, sports, fine arts, entertainment. But it is also foolish to overstress the epicurean pursuits of life and ignore such other values as selfless social service, self-sacrifice for the good of humanity, hardship and discipline in the quest of truth and God. It is in the interest of higher self-development that selfishness and egotism should be denounced. But at the same time it is also in the best interests of society that every individual should be true to himself and concentrate on the constructive development of his own potential. It is by developing oneself to the height of one's possibility that one can serve society best. So it is foolish to associate evil with self-concern. However much one may go out in the service of society, one must also have a firm basis of self-sufficiency within oneself. Spiritual unfoldment can strengthen the feeling of self-sufficiency consonantly with the spirit of self-giving. The feeling of freedom and self-sufficiency is at its strongest when the individual discovers his rootedness in the eternal.

THE NEED FOR SPIRITUAL TRAINING

Regular practice of meditation can put into the hands of man effective spiritual weapons with which to conquer depression. When an individual feels lost, his mind becomes identified with one all-engulfing feeling of depression. A person who is trained in meditation can objectify depression as a passing mental state, and thus overcome it. As he tends to fall into depression, he has the strength and power to detach himself from it. By searching analysis and self-examination, he can rise above it. By gaining insight into the causes of depression, he can dispel it. He can further divert the depressed libido into new, constructive channels. A reorientation of psychic energy would thus take place. The energy which was withdrawn from conventional pursuits may be reapplied to new goals of spiritual vision.

Meditation helps a person to discover his rootedness in the eternal. This enables him to move with the flux of change without self-estrangement. No amount of change in customs and manners, in social fashions and cultural trends, can unhinge him. No amount of change in physical ability and social status can upset him either. He realizes that every phase of life has its appropriate usefulness and meaning. Every status in life has its appropriate values. So instead of trying desperately to cling to the phase of life which is passing, he can quickly readjust himself to the next phase of life characterized by its own set of values. For example, in the evening of life, instead of trying to hang on to the youth that is slipping, he can humbly share with humanity the fruits of his life-long experience and wisdom in a way appropriate to old age. By learning to exist in the presence of the eternal, he can make his own presence a silent source of strength, solace, and inspiration to the younger generation. The disappearance of youthful vigor may witness the appearance of a new power born of mature wisdom and love.

CHAPTER III

How to Overcome Anxiety

ANXIETY IS THE MOST fundamental of all psychological problems. All mental disturbances, neurotic and psychotic, are ultimately traceable to anxiety. Many physical ailments such as insomnia, headache, heart condition, and high blood pressure have their psychical roots in anxiety. Many forms of abnormal behavior such as alcoholism, drug addiction, compulsive criminality, and juvenile delinquency are ultimately conditioned by anxiety.

Anxiety is not confined to any particular age or group of people. It is a pervasive feature of the human situation. But every age, along with new opportunities, brings its own peculiar crop of pressures and problems. New types of fear and anxiety arise in consequence. Anxiety is stirred up in new directions. Today it seems true in a special sense that we live in an age of anxiety. Modern man finds himself deeply sunk in the abyss of anxiety. He is dangerously caught between the Scylla of atomic annihilation and the Charybdis of psychic alienation and uprootedness. On the one hand the very survival of the human race and civilization is at stake. A third World War is capable of blasting the entire human species off the face of the earth. The thoughtless pressing of a few buttons would be enough to kill humanity many times over. On the other hand, modern man has been cut adrift from his traditional psycho-social and spiritual moorings. Loneliness, isolation, self-alienation, confusion due to the collapse of traditional values, have cut the solid ground from under his feet. The devastating power of nonbeing is felt vividly at the very center of his own being.

ANXIETY AND FEAR

In dealing with the problem of anxiety proper, it would be desirable to distinguish it from fear. Fear is our emotional reaction to some recognizable external danger. While walking in the street, a person sees at a short distance a tiger let loose. He becomes afraid. Since his fear has a definite object, he can try to do something about it. Either he screams so that people may come to his aid, or he runs away to take shelter in the nearest house. Or he reaches for some suitable weapon in order to defend himself against the tiger. Or if he is too weak-minded, he faints then and there, so that the awareness of the great danger, along with its unbearable nervous strain, is blotted out of his mind.

Anxiety is not attached to any definite object. It is an indefinable state of mental uneasiness or malaise which seems to be objectless. When a person in the grip of anxiety is asked what is bothering him, all he can say is, "It is nothing." So anxiety is somehow related to "nothing." It is produced by the power of nonbeing. But what is this nothing or nonbeing? According to some, the power of nonbeing is the imaginary or fictitious danger. For instance, suppose the man who was afraid of the tiger is now told by a friend that it is only a paper tiger, a vividly realistic painting. Normally his fears should immediately dissolve, because there is nothing now to be afraid of. But still, it just so happens that this man continues to be strangely afraid. He is afraid of going near or touching this paper tiger. He is afraid of nothing, but still afraid, nonetheless. His affect is irrational and meaningless. Perhaps he sees some dark, destructive forces surrounding and permeating that paper tiger. These terrific forces are of course invisible to other people. So he is afraid of something which is nothing. He is afraid of that nothing which is still something.

But is our account complete when we say that the power of nonbeing is that of imaginary danger? Why does this man imagine those dark, invisible forces? Most probably they are the projection of some unknown, dark forces buried in his unconscious mind. In that case the power of nothing can be identified as the hidden unconscious. Maybe in his childhood he had some traumatic experiences connected with a picture of a tiger. He has now no conscious memory of that experience. If, in the course of probing the past, he recollects that long-forgotten traumatic experience and emotionally relives it, it will perhaps lose its secret terror once and for all. A man afraid of a paper tiger is like "an elephant quaking at the sight of a mouse,"* as Karl Menninger puts it. The fear is irrational—out of all proportion to the external situation. It is subjectively conditioned. It is anxiety as the "dread of nothing."

But is our account complete if we say that the power of nonbeing is some hidden and unknown content of the unconscious? This is perhaps true of neurotic anxiety. But anxiety is also the experience of all perfectly

* Karl A. Menninger, *The Human Mind*, 3rd ed. (New York: Alfred A. Knopf, 1959), p. 256.

normal people. If a person says he has no worry or anxiety at all, his well-wishers have valid reason to be anxious about him. The more intelligent and sophisticated a person is, the more likely he is to experience anxiety. He becomes anxious about the fulfillment of the purpose of his own being. He has a sense of purpose, and at the same time an awareness of the negative possibility of the non-fulfillment of that purpose. As a finite being, he can never be sure about the actualization of his hidden possibilities. The more he reflects, the more he becomes aware of nonbeing as an essential element of the structure of his own existence. That is the meaning of finitude. Finite existence is compounded of being and nonbeing. Life may be cut short, the unfolding potentialities of one's existence ruthlessly damaged, the dream of life shattered in any moment by the cruel laughter of fate. Hence the deep anxiety that lies buried at the heart of existence. It is the threat of nonbeing which is an inescapable ingredient of all being.

The foregoing remarks may be summed up by saying that whereas fear has a definite object, anxiety is related to something which is nothing. It may be produced by imaginary danger, by some unknown content of the unconscious, or by the power of nonbeing inherent in existence.

TYPES OF ANXIETY

An intelligent approach to the problem of anxiety requires an understanding of the different types of anxiety. Different causes are operative in producing such different types. Today's chief theories of anxiety fasten especially upon one or another type or cause of anxiety. Broadly speaking, anxiety is of two kinds: normal or existential, and morbid or pathological. In the following pages we shall consider certain forms of anxiety and indicate the way they can be overcome.

THE FREUDIAN THEORY

Sigmund Freud's early theory of neurotic anxiety was formulated along physiological lines. Influenced by Helmholtz's concept of psychosomatic correlations, Freud was anxious to find the physiological root of anxiety. And he found that root in thwarted or inhibited sexuality. "When sexual tension arising within the body attains a certain degree, it leads in the mind to sexual desire, libido, with various accompanying ideas and emotions; but when, for any reason, this natural process is checked, the tension is transformed into anxiety."* He also toyed with another idea which has been called the toxicological theory. Under the influence of his friend Fliess, he was inclined to believe that the inhibition of the sexual function produced a toxic condition, that is to say, some disturbance in the chemistry of the body. This toxic condition was identified with the physiological root of anxiety. Another variation of his early view is known as the libido transformation theory,** positing that when strong sexual desire or libido is inhibited from fulfillment, it is transformed into anxiety.

In his later years, Freud perceived the inadequacy of his early physiological theory. Why is it that somatic-physical excitation is denied admission to the mental field and is inhibited in its expression as conscious desire? Such inhibition obviously presupposes the repres-

---

* Ernest Jones, *The Life and Work of Sigmund Freud,* Vol. I (New York: Basic Books, 1957), p. 258.
** *Ibid.,* Vol. II, p. 224.

sive agency of the psyche with a defensive aim. So a purely physiological account of neurotic anxiety is absurd. Psychic factors that thwart the sexual function must be taken into account.

Moreover, morbid anxiety understood as thwarted sexuality (or transformed libido) makes it radically different in origin from real anxiety in the face of physical danger. Real anxiety is a defensive posture of the ego. It is an expression of its instinct of self-preservation. It would be reasonable to imagine that morbid anxiety also ultimately proceeds from the ego. Freud took this logical step in his final formulation of the theory of anxiety. In his "Inhibition, Symptoms and Anxiety," he looked upon morbid anxiety as a defensive agency of the ego which is afraid of unconscious drives and impulses on account of possible social condemnation or punishment.* Some sexual impulses or aggressive instincts are repressed because the ego is anxious about the censure of the super-ego or about punishment from without. One may distinguish here between primary anxiety and secondary anxiety. Primary anxiety causes the psychic repression or inhibition of some unconscious drives. Secondary anxiety is the result of such repression. It is the accumulating inner tension reflected in the mind, without the mind having any precise knowledge of what is happening.

There is no doubt that Freud laid his finger upon a fundamental cause of pathological anxiety. The more man gains insight into the forms of repression and self-mutilation imposed by civilization, the more he can devise ways and means of overcoming pathological anxiety. Ethical and religious leaders must stop talking of sex as a reprehensible thing. It is just a natural urge

* *Ibid.*, Vol. III, p. 255.

with its legitimate function in the creative flow of life and in the psychic growth of personality. The repression of sex can succeed only in driving it into perverse and abnormal channels. The premature suppression of sex in the interest of religious goals eventually proves disastrous in spite of some apparent or real gain. It is bound to undermine one's health and one's will to live. It encourages gradual withdrawal from the social reality. It makes the external world seem illusory, because all libido has been drained from it. It reveals one's physical existence as a veritable prison-house for the soul. The desexualized person gets passionately set to flee it all—to escape from this dark dungeon of earthly existence.

The right attitude toward the unconscious drives of personality is neither ascetic suppression nor chaotic indulgence. It is an attitude of organized and intelligent self-fulfillment based on reality. In the course of organized and intelligent living, libido is likely to be transformed into a striving for higher and higher values. Our unconscious urges are often symbolized by the image of the serpent. The serpent power is not to be crushed or destroyed. It has to be tactfully transformed into a vital and essential element of integrated personality.

In Hindu mythology we are told that when the Lord Śiva was attacked by a dangerous serpent, he did not destroy it but brought it under control and put it around his neck as a shining garland. In consequence a treacherous enemy was turned into a precious friend. Similarly when Krishna found himself entangled in the dangerous coils of a huge serpent that used to live in a river, he subdued its power by dancing upon its hood. Then he redirected the serpent from the river to the ocean. In other words, he channeled the libido energy toward the fulfillment of cosmic welfare. He reoriented

the basic energy of the unconscious toward the unfoldment of cosmic consciousness, of all-embracing love
and wisdom.

Through organized fulfillment of the unconscious
psyche, libido can indeed be transformed into the pure
flame of passion for truth, righteousness, and freedom.
Destruction of the serpent—suppression of libido—may
produce supernatural strength or immensely intensified
religious fervor, but ultimately it brings about a disintegration of personality, a dissociation of the person
from nature and society.

ANXIETY AND THE TRAUMA OF BIRTH

Whereas Freud derives morbid anxiety from the
ethico-religious censorship of unconscious impulses,
Otto Rank stresses the trauma of birth as the prototype
of all anxiety. The baby is perfectly secure and comfortable in the mother's womb. At the time of birth there is
the pain of transition to the outside world. This is the
horror of exposure to the hazards of the unknown. And
the comfort and security of the mother's womb is lost.
Birth is therefore a traumatic experience. The cry of the
new-born baby well expresses this trauma. But this anxiety of separation and radical change of environment is
a necessary concomitant of the growing process of life. It
is the *sine qua non* of the emergence of the individual as
an independent entity. In the course of maturation the
individual has to go through similar experiences of
separation and radical change at the various critical
stages of life. When the child first goes to school away
from parents and home, he experiences a kind of anxiety not very dissimilar from the trauma of birth. Then
one day as a grown-up young man he may quit home

and move into the hazards of the battlefield, far, far away from all familiar surroundings. The call of duty then creates for him a new anxiety situation. Those who can take such anxiety upon themselves and face the responsibilities of life with all the strength and resources at their command, are truly brave indeed. Those who break down under the pressure of such anxiety lose the opportunity of developing inner strength of character.

The art of living implies the ability to integrate the anxiety of change, growth, and continuous rebirth. Proper training in this respect necessarily begins at the mother's knee. An overprotective mother can spoil the child. A negligent mother who is chiefly concerned with her own personal happiness, or social status, leaves the child emotionally helpless to master anxiety. It is only when the growing child is adequately nourished by love and at the same time encouraged to stand more and more upon his own feet, that anxiety ceases to be a corrosive agency. On the contrary, in the growing life of a self-confident individual, the anxiety inherent in radically new situations becomes a stimulating factor. It inspires him to the height of his ability.

It is the anxiety of change and rebirth which fosters extreme conservatism. People in the grip of such anxiety oppose all radical reforms. They turn a blind eye to the emergence of new values. They crucify those who dare to disturb the existing order. Forced into any new, strange situation, they instinctively endeavor to revert to the previous state of affairs. They are the arch enemies of innovation, initiative, and adventure.

The way to overcome the inertia or stagnation produced by anxiety is to grasp the significance of change as the stuff of life. Life is ever-new creation. It is a false sense of security that inspires one to resist change. To flow with the flux of change, and yet remain anchored in the eternal, is the secret of living. Our best security lies in our ability to move forward with the movement of time, with a clear vision of destiny. Not to be able to move forward is to get pushed backward. Anxiety can be assuaged not by holding on to the past, but by integrating the past into the present and by creatively advanc- ing into the future.

SOCIAL ANXIETY

Another type of anxiety is social anxiety. Every man is born in a certain social context, in a more or less organized community. Relationship to the social environment enters into the very essence of his being. When a person lives in conformity with the traditional norm of society, he feels a sense of security. But when, for some reason or other, there is a disturbance of his social relationship, he experiences anxiety. When he acts unethically in an ethically oriented society, he becomes anxious. When he acts ethically in an unethical society, that also makes him anxious. The root cause of such anxiety is the conflict between individual behavior and social norm. Some try to solve this problem by following the policy of unthinking conformity to the demands of the community. But is the problem really solved that way? In the process of unthinking conformity, one's own personal sense of moral values may become suppressed. And certainly one's own deep-rooted desire to affirm oneself as an individual, as a distinctive spiritual entity, as a creative source of new values, becomes ruthlessly submerged. Consequently new forms of anxiety are created. At the other extreme, some follow the path of open rebellion, of protest and nonconformity. They are animated by the ideal of individual self-affirmation, regardless of social reaction. The growing volume of social opprobrium and oppression may tend to crush them. Social ostracism may gradually drive them into extreme isolation and loneliness, if not to the verge of madness. The impact of all this cannot but intensify anxiety to the utmost.

It is evident from the foregoing that whichever way a person may turn in molding his relationship to society, there is bound to be anxiety in some form or other. A total elimination of anxiety is more than can be expected. Part of the training of life is to increase one's ability to tolerate anxiety. The balanced ideal of life is to keep in mind two important things in making decisions: (1) the total welfare and progress of society and of mankind; and (2) maximum self-affirmation as an agency of higher spiritual values and ultimate human welfare. The more the person succeeds in engineering his life accordingly, the more anxiety is transmuted from a corrosive force into a stimulating factor. That which threatens mental equilibrium becomes an ingredient of mental growth.

EXISTENTIAL ANXIETY

Existentialist thinkers such as Kierkegaard, Heidegger, Sartre, Paul Tillich and others have written a good deal about anxiety as an existential category. It is not merely an uneasy and fearful feeling caused by the changing circumstances of life. Existential anxiety is a type of anxiety which is rooted in the very existence of man. It is inescapable and unavoidable. The more a person becomes aware of the essential structure of existence, the more this kind of anxiety is stirred up. One can eliminate this anxiety only by denying life itself. Life-denying philosophers have tried to lift man out of existential anxiety in the name of the transcendent and timeless spirit. The spirit has been affirmed as the sublime negation of life with all its chance and change, and its hazard and horror.

But those who wish to accept life with all its hazard and horror, along with its boundless promise and glory, must accept anxiety as an essential ingredient of existence. It cannot be separated from life, but can be made to serve the purpose of life as a source of stimulation and inward strength. One can take anxiety upon oneself and move forward with the creative adventure of life.

There are two essential characteristics of human existence: finitude and freedom. As a finite entity, man emerges out of nothingness, and steadily and inescapably heads toward nothingness. Every step he takes forward in life is also a step towards death. His whole life is like a gay bubble that makes a brief noise on the surface of the swift current of time. It is a brief interval of light between two unfathomable realms of darkness. His life is exposed on all sides to the threat of nonbeing. Contingency is writ large across the face of the world in which he lives. Anything may happen any moment in this world. As he steps out of his home, crosses the street, rides in an automobile or aeroplane, a sudden accident may strike him down. Political brush fires, ever present around the globe, may at any time erupt into a global catastrophe, reducing civilization to a shambles. Even when a person is peacefully asleep in his own home, nobody can tell what may happen to his sweet nest of security. A sudden earthquake or a wanton act of incendiarism may suddenly reduce his safety to a mockery. Even when one outlasts all such hazards and untoward happenings, the cruel hand of death is sure to snatch him away one day. Nothing can stop this ultimate decree of nonbeing. The intensity of existential anxiety is in direct proportion to the awareness of finitude and contingency of life. So Dr. Tillich rightly observed: "Anxiety is finitude, experienced as one's own finitude."* It is "the existential awareness of nonbeing."

ANXIETY AND FREEDOM

Another essential characteristic of man is his freedom. Of all the living creatures, man is born the most helpless, because he is born with a very flexible nervous system. But in this very helplessness does also lie his glory. He is born with a tremendous potential. He has the ability to make or mar his future. He has the possibility within him to rise to the height of divine glory by creatively expressing such higher values as truth, beauty, justice, freedom, love. But he also has the possibility of descending to the level of the brute, or even lower than the brutish. Senseless cruelty and devilish destruction surpassing that of most ferocious animals may be his. Such brutal possibility is the implication of the freedom that is man's. Anxiety is born of reflection upon the possibilities of freedom.

It has been observed that anxiety is "the dizziness of freedom."** When a person chances to look down into the yawning abyss of his worst possibility, he becomes dizzy with anxiety or dread. It is possible for him to squander his spiritual potential and violate the inner sanctuary of his soul. It is possible for him to regress to

* Paul Tillich, *The Courage to Be* (New Haven: Yale University Press, 1959), p. 35.
** Søren Kierkegaard, *The Concept of Dread*, Walter Lowrie, trans. (Princeton: Princeton University Press, 1957), p. 55.

the perverted or walk into the trap of the diabolical. It is also possible for him to encompass a thoughtless abortion of the higher possibilities of his nature.

Freedom also produces anxiety as a sequel to the sense of responsibility it generates. When we freely choose a task such as the founding of a family or the serving of a social institution, we feel the responsibility for our chosen action. We may have to fight against odds. We may have to mobilize resources against much enmity and opposition. We have to carefully weigh in the balance how our various actions are going to affect the weal and woe of other people. This constant uneasiness naturally lies upon the head that wears responsibility. Considerable emotional stress is generated. This encourages the tendency to escape from freedom. Such an escape is the line of least resistance. But it reflects emotional immaturity. It is by boldly accepting responsibility and by taking upon oneself the resulting anxiety, that a strong and mature personality emerges.

In escaping from freedom a person turns away from his authentic potentiality of self-existence or Being-in-the-world.* In avoiding the anxiety of freedom, he follows the crowd and loses himself in the crowd. He gets lost in the anonymous mass life. He is steeped in the immediacy of inauthentic being. This cannot but produce another kind of anxiety, the anxiety of spiritual death. Man's desire to develop as a unique spiritual entity is too deep-rooted to be ignored. Complete suppression of this desire produces the anxiety of self-alienation from which one cannot save oneself. But by accepting the anxiety of gradual self-development and creative

* Martin Heidegger, *Existence and Being*, Werner Brocks, trans. (Chicago: Henry Regnery Company, 1949), p. 16.

freedom, one can transform anxiety into the energy of creative self-fulfillment.

Growing spiritual insight can nullify the corrosive influence of anxiety. It can effectively turn the anxiety of freedom into the joy of inward fullness.

ANXIETY AND NESCIENCE

The root cause of anxiety working as a negative force is ontological ignorance. It is what Vedānta calls primal ignorance or nescience (*avidyā*). It is the ignorance of one's authentic self and its relationship to Being. It is the ignorance of, or alienation from, that nontemporal dimension of existence (*turīya*) in which the individual and the universal are essentially one. The seers of the Upaniṣads declare that awareness of the nontemporal dimension of Being helps man to conquer all fear and anxiety.

There is an old Vedāntic story illustrating how the brave man becomes a coward through ignorance. An old laundryman who was half blind was in the habit of taking his laundry to the riverside every day upon the back of his favorite donkey. One day he had an unusually heavy load of laundry. By the time he was through with the washing and drying of all clothes, it had become pretty dark. The worried old man, who could hardly see at night, was calling his donkey thus: "Where are you, my pet, it is so dark now. I am not so afraid of lions and tigers as I am afraid of night." Just at that moment it so happened that there was a lion in a nearby bush. The lion heard the words. The lion thought that night must be some kind of terrible monster, far more powerful than himself. And so he became afraid. The laundryman, who was looking for his donkey, heard a rustle in the bush and placed his load of laundry upon the lion's back, thinking that it was his donkey.

Seized with extreme fear and anxiety, the lion thought that this must be the terrible monster, Night, who had already appeared upon the scene. So the lion meekly submitted to the laundryman's driving him to his house. The lion-donkey was tied in the stable and the laundryman retired for the night. On the following day before the break of dawn the laundryman, according to his custom, put together another load of dirty clothes, placed the bundle upon the back of the "donkey," and proceeded to the riverside, the "donkey" walking behind him. The sun was just rising now. The veil of darkness was being lifted from the face of the earth. Another lion appeared in the neighborhood and witnessed the procession of the old laundryman and his faithful "donkey." With a feeling of shame, he shouted to his kin and said: "Hey, what are you doing there? Acting like a donkey?" The lion-donkey answered in a whisper: "Hush—don't talk so loud. Here is the terrible monster called Night. If you shout and brag, the monster will capture you in no time and break your neck." Undaunted by this, the lion said: "Is that so? Let us see what happens if you follow my advice. Give out a good roaring sound and declare your identity." The "donkey" followed the advice and lifted his voice in a thunderous roar. The laundryman was now startled to hear the roaring of the lion. He looked back and was horrified to see what he saw. Summoning all his courage and strength, he ran away from the place as fast as he could, leaving behind his laundry and all. The lion was instantly released from the donkey-spell and with a majestic bound went back to his own domain of freedom.

This is a story about the kind of ignorance that casts a hypnotic spell and turns a lion into a donkey—i.e., puts the chains of bondage around the neck of freedom. The fear of night made the lion a coward. And what is night? It symbolizes nothingness—the monster of ignorance. It symbolizes anxiety which has been aptly described as "the shapeless daughter of the shapeless night."

It is within the power of man to break loose from the shackles of the past and to carve out a new path of self-development. It is in his power to rise above the threatening conspiracy of circumstances and to remold his environment in accordance with his inward sense of values. Endless talk about determinism makes him forget his spiritual essence and regard himself as a plaything of chance circumstances, a helpless log of wood drifting on the tide of events. The social monster of "Thou shalt not" stares him in the face. Ceaseless suggestions about "should" and "should not" transform his existence into a socially and politically manipulatable object—turning the lion into a donkey.

The spirit in man is essentially rooted in the eternal—the nontemporal dimension of existence—where fear and doubt, death and destruction, cowardice and bondage, are unknown. Primal ignorance in the form of self-oblivion or self-estrangement uproots him from his ground of existence. So long as man is in the realm of ignorance, anxiety torments him, no matter what he does. If he lives in forgetfulness of higher spiritual values, he sinks in the abyss of unknown fears. By turning a blind eye to his higher spiritual potential or by smothering the voice of the infinite within him, he loses himself. Suppression of that voice produces what Kierkegaard has called the anxiety of paganism.

But if, in paganism, there is latent anxiety due to

alienation from the spirit, in Christianity there is patent anxiety due to the sense of sinfulness and obsession with the devil. Paganism is immersion in the immediate, in the givenness of nature. Christianity swings back to the opposite extreme of alienation from the immediate, from the solid support of nature. The more a man turns to God, the more his latent anxieties come to the fore on account of fear of the dark forces in life. This may be called the anxiety of religious longing. It is the anxiety of estrangement from one's instinctual base in life.

Anxiety is effectively overcome when the veil of ignorance is lifted—when the individual is integrated with the ultimate ground of existence. He then becomes aware of his inmost self as a higher principle of unity, bringing together, in a harmonious whole, both nature and spirit. In this dynamic self-realization, the immediacy of instinct and the mediation of reason become integrated. Various impulses and desires get organized with reference to the central goal of life. Blissful realization of the eternal opens up new directions in which the instinctual drives of personality can be fruitfully channeled.

CHAPTER IV

How to Rise Above Despair

THE PROBLEM OF DESPAIR goes much deeper than that of depression. Depression, dejection, grief, and the like are afflictions of the mind. They may pass away without reaching the point of despair. Despair seems somehow to affect the very central core of human existence. Depression is an emotional disturbance, a more or less transient sickness of the mind. Despair is a sickness of the soul, an affliction of the inmost being.

Despair is the condition of extreme hopelessness, when even the last hope of man's life, the hope of death, is gone. So Kierkegaard has described it as the "sickness unto death." Sickness unto death is different from mortal or fatal sickness. Suppose a man is suffering from tuberculosis or cancer and is told by doctors that there is no hope of recovery. His sickness is fatal, but still it may not affect his spirit. He may be ready to embrace death with a smiling face. He may consider death to be only the gateway to a higher mode of existence of the spirit—to life everlasting. So his fatal sickness is not the kind of sickness unto death that despair is. When a man is in despair, he lives to experience death, "dying the death."*

* Søren Kierkegaard, *Fear and Trembling,* and *Sickness Unto Death* (Garden City: Doubleday and Company, 1954), p. 151.

When a person is afraid of dying, he busies himself living. The joy of hurried living fills his days. When a person is afraid of living, he wants to die. Death brings hope into his life and provides an escape from the pain of living. But when a person finds both life and death meaningless, he is in despair. The door of life is closed to him, because life has lost for him all warmth and color, all meaning and purpose. The door of death is closed to him also, because he finds it no solution to his problems. Desire to die is felt to be no less sacrilegious than sinful living. Thus the despairing person finds himself in the darkest dungeon of no-exit.

Despair is fundamentally a spiritual problem. An individual may be in extremely adverse circumstances, having to fight against overwhelming odds, but still he may be free from despair. On the contrary, an individual may be well adjusted in society, rolling in wealth and luxury, but still he may be in despair. Something indefinable is eating into his vitals. An individual may be outwardly very happy and cheerful, but underlying his jovial front there may be a deep undercurrent of despair. It is not so much conditioned by outward circumstances. It has its roots deep down in one's soul. Consequently it is an especially human problem, whether people are aware of it or not. Those who are not aware of it are too much absorbed in the material pursuits of life. The more aware a person becomes of his spiritual nature, of his deeper potentiality, of his relationship to the eternal, the more despair comes to the front. The more a person suffers from the stings of despair, the more he may be on his way to higher spiritual fulfillment. Spiritual progress brings with it the sense of despair. Those who have no conscious feeling of despair are in a sense spiritually dead. Despair contains an element of what Plato called "divine discontent." It is this discontent—the profound sense of dissatisfaction with the status quo of socialized existence—which is the beginning of higher spiritual growth.

Can despair actually be described as a sickness of the spirit? That would depend on what is meant by the spirit. The word "spirit" is sometimes used to mean the element of pure transcendence in human existence. In this sense it is what is called in Hindu philosophy the Self (*ātman or puruṣa*). It is pure being and pure consciousness; it is the nontemporal dimension of existence. Understood in this sense, the spirit knows no sickness. It is eternal bliss. It is beyond pain and pleasure, joy and sorrow, health and sickness, which are characteristics of our psycho-physical existence. The changing conditions of the mind-body complex do not affect the pure spirit. If the spirit is fire and the body is iron, the mind is like a piece of red-hot iron aglow from its contact with fire. The spirit in its pure essence transcends all emotional fluctuations, all psychosomatic disturbances. Man's deepest potentiality lies in his ability to live a life of the spirit. Alienation from his spiritual essence lies at the root of despair.

But the word "spirit" may be used in another sense. In the sense indicated above, the spirit is the nontemporal dimension of existence. It is the ultimate ground of being. It is the ultimate source of all knowledge and joy. But in the second sense, the spirit is the mind insofar as it is illuminated by some degree of apprehension of the nontemporal. It is what is popularly called man's higher nature. It is his refined and transparent nature (*sāttvic prakṛti*), whereas in the former sense the spirit is no-nature, no-attribute, no-mind. In the first sense man lives in the medium of the spirit. In the latter sense, the spirit is the characteristic of man: it is his mind animated by his glimpse of the eternal and a consequent vision of higher values. But the mind may also function in complete oblivion of the eternal. It may catch a fleeting glimpse of the eternal and then again lose it. Its momentary illumination may be followed by a plunge into deep darkness. Since the mind can never completely grasp the nontemporal Being in its integral fullness, since the eternal is a radically different dimension of Being, underlying all the knowledge and achievement of the mind there is always bound to be a feeling of doubt, an incorrigible sense of inadequacy and imperfection. Herein lies the central core of despair. Despair may thus be defined, as Kierkegaard does, as a sickness of the spirit, when the word spirit is used in the sense of the mind as related to the eternal. But be it noted here again that in the sense of the eternal itself the spirit is essentially beyond all sickness and despair.

Man cannot be his true self without active awareness of his relationship to the ground of existence—the eternal—because his essence lies in this relationship. His self is a synthesis of the finite and the infinite—of the temporal and the nontemporal. He has the ability to cognize this relationship and to reconstruct himself on the basis thereof. This ability is his higher spiritual nature. So long as he lives in utter forgetfulness of his relationship with the eternal, he is in despair. Such forgetfulness constitutes a suppression of his deeper possibilities, a profanation of his soul's inner sanctuary. The more he becomes aware of his essential relationship to the eternal, the more he experiences the mixed feelings of joy and despair, of excitement and separation. His joy knows no bounds as he becomes aware of his identity as a dynamic focus of the Supreme Being. But at the same time his sorrow also is deepened. A painful sense of separation from the Supreme is keenly felt. Hitherto separation, though a fact, was not felt. Now separation, having appeared in consciousness, becomes a painful experience. His joyful sense of rootedness in the eternal is accompanied by the painful feeling of alienation from the eternal. A deepening sense of frustration comes with the realization that no amount of human effort can bridge the gulf between the finite and the infinite, between the temporal existence and the nontemporal. Thus despair as sickness of the spirit is immensely intensified.

CONSCIOUS AND UNCONSCIOUS DESPAIR

But still, from the standpoint of spiritual fulfillment, potentiated and enlightened despair is far better than suppressed and unconscious despair. Unconscious despair is spiritual death—utter oblivion of man's divine heritage. Conscious despair, with all its terrible sufferings, is a necessary phase of the process of self-transcendence. Unconscious despair is a sickness of the spirit, because it is obscuration of man's higher nature, his latent sense of higher values, his hidden possibility of conscious union with the eternal. Conscious despair also is sickness of the spirit, because it imposes profound suffering upon the spiritual seeker. It is the agonizing sense of separation from the infinite. It is like the vertigo that one experiences while looking down into a fathomless abyss or up at a towering mountain peak. But still this is a kind of sickness that can be radically cured. It is cured when its hidden cause, the basic ontological ignorance (*avidyā*) is removed. It is good that in the course of the intensification of our awareness of the eternal, despair comes to the surface with all its dark terror. That is when we can effectively deal with it and conquer it.

It has been noted that the sense of despair is immensely accentuated when a man stands before God. But this is true only when a person stands before God existentially. Otherwise there need be no despair and no sense of sin. A person may stand before God aesthetically or poetically. In that case God as the truth, the good, and the beautiful exists in the medium of imagination. Beautiful, aesthetic representations of the majestic grandeur of the Divine are made. Poetic vision of the glory of God comes alive in rich resonance and rhythm of language. But in spite of such aesthetic representation of the Divine, the poet may be totally unconcerned about his personal relationship to the Divine. He may, by his power of creative imagination, abstract from his own personal existence. He poetizes perfection from the impersonal standpoint of aesthetic contemplation. However self-contradictory his personal life may be, however turbulent his inner emotional conflicts, he can soar above these on the wings of creative fantasy, and play ball with the gods on the Olympic heights.

A person may also stand before God speculatively or metaphysically. In that case God is either the Form of the Good, or the ultimate unifying and explanatory principle of the given world. God is either the conceptual synthesis of all higher values, or the conceptual unity of the actual world. In either case the speculative philosopher abstracts from his own concrete existence, in his detached contemplation of the totality of being. He adopts the impersonal standpoint of abstract thinking. All the concrete items of experience, including his own individual being, are derived from his all-comprehensive system of ideas. He places himself on such a high altitude that the inner discrepancies of his personal life do not bother him. His failings in human relations can hardly reach him where he is engaged in the Olympic Game of encircling the world with ideas. He conceptualizes perfection from the impersonal standpoint of abstract speculation. He functions in the medium of conceptual thinking. He does not bother to live in the categories of his thought. The pathos of life evaporates at the cold touch of speculation. The individual's problem of existence as an individual is crushed under the conceptual steamroller.

DESPAIR AND EXISTENTIAL ENCOUNTER WITH GOD

When a person stands existentially before God, his personal life is exposed in all its nakedness. One cannot hide anything before the all-penetrating eye of cosmic consciousness. The inner discrepancies of life come to the surface. One becomes aware of one's potentialities and hidden assets. One becomes aware of one's serious limitations and handicaps, one's crimes, one's neglect of life's chances and opportunities. Existential relationship to divine perfection makes one feel like he is dust and ashes. The divine measure of perfection is like the powerful shaft of a searchlight that lays bare the nothingness of the individual. Is there any hope of realizing perfection in finite form? Is there any hope of bridging the gulf between the finite and infinite? Can the finite be ever one with the infinite? If not, imperfection belongs to the very essence of human existence. Awareness of this fact accentuates despair to the utmost.

Kierkegaard believed that however imperfect and sinful man might be, he can be saved by the power of faith.

In his view the essence of sin lies not in finitude or imperfection. Nor does it lie in criminality. It lies in lack of faith. The opposite of sin is not virtue, as paganism holds, but faith. To be imperfect is human. To make mistakes and commit crimes is also human. Sin lies in giving assent to crime and not accepting divine forgiveness. God was born to expiate human acts of sinfulness and to give tangible proof of divine love and forgiveness. When man accepts this forgiveness, then he attains salvation. He is restored to a state of harmony with God. In order to achieve such rapprochement, he has to believe in divine forgiveness. He has to believe that God's suffering was sufficient atonement for the sins of man. He has to believe that God is eager to accept and love the individual human being in spite of all his weakness, imperfection, and sinfulness. When an individual says that in spite of divine forgiveness he, himself, is unable to forget and forgive his heinous crime, he betrays his pride, egotism, and lack of faith. In consequence, at the prompting of his ego, he turns away from the door of salvation, and confirms himself further in defiant sinfulness. He sinks deeper into the despair of defiance. It is his lack of faith which drives him into despair. The affirmation of faith in Christ's love and forgiveness can make a world of difference—can pull him into the light of salvation out of the darkness of despair.

Kierkegaard's solution to the problem of despair does not differ much from the position of Christian orthodoxy. It is presented in the garb of theological dogma. The faith that has the power to save is charged with a definite mythical content. A particular historical individual—Jesus Christ—must be accepted as the only begotten Son of God. God offers forgiveness to man only

through him. The heavenly Father takes upon Himself
the consequence of human sin in the shape of His beloved Son's crucifixion. All this is consciously or unconsciously designed to have the effect of investing Christianity with celestial authority. It can certainly offer
spiritual comfort and ease to the unquestioning be-
liever. It enables him to adjust himself to his sinfulness
on the strength of the assurance of divine forgiveness.
But such faith can work only so long as myth can serve
as truth in the intellectual life of an individual. In the
case of the orthodox Christian, the Christological dogma
is the content of his redeeming faith. Devout Moslems
experience a similar kind of salvation through the acceptance of Mohammed as the greatest messenger of
God on earth. Devout Hindus may find their religious
liberation through the acceptance of Krishna as the
most perfect incarnation of God on earth. Devout Bud-
dhists may likewise experience emancipation from sin
and suffering through the acceptance of the Buddha as
the embodiment of the eternal and of the spirit of universal compassion. The dogmas of different religions
may differ. Myths may vary. But the underlying pattern
of religious solution to the problem of guilt and sin is
the same. The doctrine of divine love and forgiveness
enables the sinner to be self-adjusted in spite of his sinfulness. As one accepts divine forgiveness, one accepts
oneself as an object of divine love. Through the love of
God one learns to participate in the glory of God.

It is amazing how a brilliant dialectician like Kierkegaard betrayed emotional immaturity. Loss of his father
created an abysmal void in his emotional life. Information about the sin of his father shocked him into the
conviction that the curse of God was upon the whole
family. It was therefore not for him to live a normal life

of happiness and social success. Puritanical ideas about the sinfulness of sex and romance produced in him a spirit of rebellion against Nature. No wonder, then, that his relationship with his fiancée had little chance of blooming into fullblown love and marriage. With the emotional void gaping within him, he was desperately in search of a father image. His search was rewarded with the discovery of the doctrine of the only begotten Son. With faithful acceptance of divine forgiveness, sin and despair can now easily turn into blessed rapprochement with the heavenly Father.

SALVATION WITHOUT MYTH

Let us now see if the problem of despair can be solved without any recourse to dogma and myth. When a man existentially stands before God, his despair is naturally potentiated. On the one hand he falls infinitely short of the ideal of perfection. On the other hand many latent potentialities of his nature are found to have been neglected, and many drawbacks and shortcomings come to his attention. Measured by the standard of divine perfection, they naturally appear the blackest. But why cry over the impossible? Why reach out for the unnatural? Why shed inconsolable tears over limitations which are natural and inescapable? Why strive for absolute freedom where man, as a finite being, is necessarily entitled only to limited freedom? Why assume absolute responsibility for those events in life over which man can have little control? Why prematurely rebel against nature and create thereby a sense of being uprooted and estranged? Is it not sheer perfectionism and an unnatural way of living which calls for sanctimonious fictions in order to gain the peace of the soul?

The ideal of absolute self-perfection is the projection of an infantile desire. It is the demand of an infantile mind which cannot function except under the protection of an all-powerful, all-wise, and all-good father. God does not demand perfection from man. Perfection in finite form is a contradiction in terms. It is like the ever-receding horizon that always eludes one's grasp. True, man has it within his power always to advance and make progress, always to improve himself and his condition of living. But he can never embody perfection in his finite form. He can never touch the horizon. Insight into this human condition of finitude is the first important step in the conquest of despair. Man is ever-perfectible but never perfect. This imperfect perfectibility, this perpetually self-improving imperfection, is of the essence of his inescapable finitude.

Man's perfectibility is derived from the fact that he has unsuspected possibilities hidden within himself. The ideals that inspire him flow from a vague awareness of latent possibilities. Despair measures the distance between the actual and the ideal. But despair may turn into persevering and constructive effort in proportion to one's ability to temper idealism with realism. A realistic estimate of one's dynamic potential is of great importance. A realistic appraisal of the inescapable limitations of one's given nature and situation in the world has a sobering effect. Man has no doubt a great power to change his environment, to remold his circumstances. But there is a limit to that power. It is often tragic to ignore these limits and to harbor the delusion of grandeur and divine omnipotence. Wisdom consists in perceiving the limit and the necessity imposed by it, along with the inherent power and possibilities. Such wisdom can transmute despair into daring—into fearless espousal of new undertakings. It also turns corrosive repentance into fruitful adventure. There is no use crying uncontrollably over what one might have been or might have done. The retrospective glance which reveals the past errors and perversions belongs to a person who is already different from the person who committed them. The repentant self has already outgrown the delinquent self. A healthy attitude toward life is an objective analysis of our past mistakes and lapses with a view to profiting from them. Having gained the right insight from the happenings of the past, one should allow the past to bury itself. Morbid preoccupation with the past, whether in its sinfulness or its joyfulness, is a great hindrance to the growth of personality. After the past has delivered its lessons, let it go. Let an active vision of the future invigorate the present. Let a sober concern with the living present activate it in the direction of the future.

The final conquest of despair comes from a spiritual source. As has been indicated before, the root cause of despair lies in man's alienation from his ultimate ground of existence. The ultimate ground of existence is the Supreme Being. The roots of his life are laid deep down there. It is what a modern psychologist has called "the sustaining dimension of existence."* Vedānta calls it *turīya*, the transcendent. It is that which permeates and sustains all the known phases of experience such as waking, dreaming, and sleep, and yet transcends them all. It is the abode of bliss and beatitude. It is the abode of egoless consciousness and cosmic love. Awareness of the sustaining, nontemporal dimension of existence is shattering to all doubt and despair. It dispels all dark-

* Ira Progoff, *Depth Psychology and Modern Man* (New York: The Julian Press, 1959), pp. 261, 276.

ness by the power of light and joy. It transforms mere faith in God into personal realization of His living presence. In the nontemporal dimension, man and God are united without loss of their distinctiveness. Suffused with the joy of integration with the nontemporal, an individual can participate in life freely and spontaneously, in a spirit of love that makes no demand and expects no reward.

CHAPTER V

How to Make Decisions

THE ABILITY TO MAKE decisions is a most important factor in the growth of personality. A man is born alone, and he dies alone. And in the same way he has to grow up alone from the roots of his own being. He has to work out his own salvation or creative self-fulfillment.

In the process of physical growth a living being constantly draws elements of nourishment from his physical environment. He eats food, drinks water, absorbs light, breathes air. Others may help him in procuring these vital needs, but he has to do his own chewing and digesting and assimilating. Similarly in the process of inward spiritual growth, a person has to draw elements of nourishment from his cultural and spiritual environment. Others help him by furnishing keys to available spiritual treasures. Parents, teachers, and prophets help him in his exploration of the boundless realm of values, but he has to do his own selection, assimilation, and creative self-expression. In one word, he has to do his own self-developing. The ability to make decisions according to the purpose and potentiality of one's own being is the most essential factor in constructive and meaningful growth. This is what the Buddha meant when, at the time of his departure, he gave out to his disciples as his parting message: "Be a light unto yourself (*Ātmadipo bhava*)."

The capacity to function as a light unto oneself is the most essential characteristic of spiritual unfoldment. It is the source of one's strength of character. It is the secret of mature adulthood.

Among many grievously erroneous notions of spirituality is the belief that a spiritual person must be selfless to the extent that he must have no independent view or decision of his own, must be a mere echo of some accepted religious authority, whether the Pope or the guru. To tell the truth, this is not spirituality but infantile religiosity. In the name of religious obedience and surrender, it hinders the growth of personality. It stifles the stirring of the creative seed that lies hidden in the soul of man. In the name of God this encourages the infantile tendency of the immature to feel perfectly secure and comfortable under the protective wing of some kind of parental authority.

The essence of spirituality lies in developing to the full one's inward vision of truth and beauty and cosmic welfare. It is like kindling the torch of one's soul from the infinite Light that creatively sustains all life. Once the creative spark leaps into a steady flame, a man shines as a light unto himself and unto the world. He is now in a position to make decisions in response to the changing situations of life. And he makes his decisions independently in accordance with his inward vision of truth. Independent and enlightened decision is the mark of his transition from pseudo-religious infantilism to spiritual maturity.

As a person advances through life, every now and then he is called upon to make decisions. Sometimes decisions seem to be made almost unconsciously in the depth of his being. Later on he may become reflectively aware of his relatively unconscious decisions. For instance, a little child may have at the back of his mind a vague idea about his style of living. He may have an unconscious image of his future. So he dreams about Julius Caesar or Alexander the Great. Or, he may dream about Christ or Buddha. Or he may dream about some famous movie star or baseball hero. His lifelong striving may be secretly molded, successfully or unsuccessfully, by the unconscious decision about his style of living. Or, it may happen that when he learns to reflect upon himself, his unconscious self-image is either rejected or radically changed in the light of his revised self-estimate. He makes a new, fruitful decision on the basis of his authentic insight into himself and his life situation.

THE HARMFULNESS OF HASTY DECISIONS

Sometimes a person suffers from the evil consequences of hasty decisions. Hastily made decisions are likely to need to be hastily undone again.

A young man feels that it is time for him to get married. So he decides to marry that unusually beautiful girl whom he met the other day at a cocktail party. But he has known her only briefly. He knows little about her cultural and family background. He knows little about her ideals and ambitions in life. But what does that matter? Did she not look a paragon of beauty that evening? Was she not the life of the party? Did she not show great interest in him? That should be enough. So marriage takes place. But in the course of a year or two comes bitter disillusionment. Serious temperamental differences come out into the open. Psychic incompatibility reduces physical charm to an insignificant factor. Each begins to suspect the love and loyalty of the other. So the inevitable happens—a breakdown in communication, resulting in divorce.

Now there are people who seem to follow the same pattern of hasty decisions followed by sudden reversals. The vicious circle of the making and the breaking of decisions is thus set in motion. There are some people who are always changing their jobs, their apartments, or their partners. When a new job comes along, it appears to be just right—just the kind of job one was looking for. After a while disenchantment sets in. The search for a better job—for the really right one—begins afresh. In this way one may unhappily go on searching for the perfect way of one's life. As the new always gets old, the quest of novelty becomes a ceaseless process. Every now and then the perfect appears in some fresh form. But as soon as the freshness wears off, the illusion of perfection breaks like a soap bubble.

Various factors may contribute to the making of hasty decisions. Whenever a decision is made on superficial grounds, it proves disappointing. A young girl decides to marry a man because she is in urgent need of getting away from her family environment—the sooner the better. Here the pressure of some unfortunate circumstances becomes for her the deciding factor. The compulsion of circumstance blinds her to more vital considerations: the character and background of the person chosen. In some cases physical charm is considered decisive enough. Sometimes a young man decides to accept a job because it will yield him maximum financial gain. Later on he may feel extremely unhappy in the job and quit. He may find that financial advantage notwithstanding, the job is quite incongruous with his abiding sense of values. He made a big mistake by allowing the question of wages to be his overriding consideration. Or, perhaps he took the job in order to please his father. He is likely to find that paternal approval may not be quite relevant to the real happiness of one's own life.

Sometimes again people make hasty decisions because they are incapable of enduring the strain of indecision for any length of time. Authentic decisions may take some time to mature. This is specifically true with regard to such vital issues of life as the course of studies or the kind of training to pursue, the type of job to select, the kind of life partner to choose, the kind of environment in which to live. One must contemplate carefully the various possibilities of one's life situation. One has also to make a realistic estimate of the assets and liabilities of one's personality. All that requires time. Time is like a bull with which we have to fight as we advance through life, developing strength and attaining manhood. As we subdue time it functions as our medium of self-expression, as our instrument of new creation. But most people wish to avoid this encounter with time. Instead they wish to drift without worry on the tide of time. They shudder to halt time for the sake of soul-searching or thinking consideration of things. They prefer to be swept along by the habit of hasty decision made instantaneously on superficial grounds. The result is inauthentic living with a growing sense of inner emptiness.

THE PROBLEM OF INDECISION

Just as at one extreme there are people who are in the habit of making hasty decisions, at the other extreme

there are people who seem to suffer from chronic indecision. They are perpetually sitting on the fence. They
just cannot muster sufficient strength to commit themselves to any definite line of action. They are perpetually vacillating or floating on clouds of endless possibility. The prospect of landing upon the *terra firma* of the
actual scares them to death.

This mental condition of indecision is often occa-
sioned by unresolved inner conflicts. Some people can
never make up their minds whether they should belong
to any political party or not, whether they should belong to any religious organization or not, whether they
should settle down to any particular sphere of action or
not. One part of their nature is inclined toward striking
their roots somewhere, having a sense of belonging
somewhere. But another part of their nature rebels
against all forms of self-limitation, and yearns to keep
flying in the boundless realm of the possible. Now this
and now that tendency may gain ascendency, but never
does any one of them gain a decisive victory. A happy
compromise between such conflicting tendencies requires a certain degree of courage and self-understand-
ing.

Prolonged indecision may be due to an extreme fear
of risk and responsibility. There is an unavoidable element of risk in any line of action that is chosen. It is the
risk of displeasing somebody or stepping upon somebody's toes. It is the risk of losing something or under-
going some hardship. And since most of our decisions
and actions are likely to affect some fellow being directly or indirectly, they bring on a sense of responsibility. Those who are emotionally immature and weak in
character shudder to take risks and assume responsibility. They are afraid of displeasing anybody. They recoil

from the prospect of discomfort and hardship. But life is not always a bed of roses. Even when it *is* a bed of roses, sharp thorns go along with them. Life often challenges us to a choice between equally unpleasant alternatives. When we accept the challenge, whatever we do is bound to involve risk, rigor, and responsibility. If we run away from the challenge, we lose the opportunity for growth. In shirking responsibility we may follow the line of least resistance, but we commit psychological and spiritual suicide.

The state of indecision may also be due to the absence of any deciding principle or criterion in our mental equipment. Intelligent decision implies a determinate principle. The psychological root of all deciding principles is one's self-image or sense of identification. In early childhood the groundwork for one's self-identification is laid. A child unconsciously identifies himself either with the father, or with the mother, or with both. If he identifies himself with the father, the ideas, beliefs, and emotional attitudes of the father are unconsciously absorbed. A masculine self-image is thus in the making. If he identifies himself with the mother, the ideals, beliefs, and emotional attitudes of the mother are unconsciously absorbed, and a feminine self-image develops. If he identifies himself with both parents, a composite self-image is in the making. In accordance with varying measures of nearness to, and admiration for, the distinctive personalities of the parents, a child's self-image incorporates within itself, in a certain constellation, both masculine and feminine characteristics.

But under certain circumstances a child may be left without the opportunity of identifying himself with either one of the parents. This happens especially when the parents use the child in their frequent bickering with one another. They bestow favors or frowns upon the child quite arbitrarily. They punish or reward the child arbitrarily, that is, not in accordance with the quality and conduct of the child, but in accordance with the changing emotional needs and conflicts of their own lives. In a situation like this, the child becomes extremely confused, both emotionally and ideologically. He is left hanging in the air without any feeling of self-identification. He cannot develop any clear sense of values. He hardly knows where he stands or what he should do. No clear self-image nourished by higher values has a chance of growing within him. He is deprived of a clear sense of identity. He does not seem to know who he is. As a result, he lacks the basis upon which to make any clear-cut decisions in life.

VARIOUS PRINCIPLES OF DECISION

The foregoing discussion brings us to the question of different principles of decision. Lack of self-identification in early childhood induces the state of indecision. On the contrary, pronounced self-identification generates various deciding principles. Some of these principles may be very inadequate and superficial. Adoption of such principles naturally cannot be conducive to the mature growth of personality. Fortunate is the individual who grows up with a sound and adequate principle of decision gradually taking shape within him. A sound principle of decision is the greatest asset of personality. It is the ultimate source of abiding happiness and authentic self-fulfillment.

The principle of pleasure, the principle of perfection, the principle of authority, the principle of non-limitation—these are all more or less inadequate and imperfect criteria. A brief consideration of such principles will be in order before we proceed to outline the most adequate deciding principle. The principle which is most commonly used as the basis of decision is the pleasure principle. This means that the universal natural tendency is to choose that which is most pleasurable, and to avoid that which is unpleasant and disagreeable. For instance, people are usually inclined to choose foods which are most palatable, such as fancy desserts, creams or sweetmeats. But an intelligent person soon learns that the pleasant is not always the best. Items of food chosen mainly on the ground of their pleasure value may prove ruinous to health by producing obesity and by depriving the person of such essential ingredients of health as vitamins, minerals, and proteins. In the best interest of health, strength, and longevity, one may find it reasonable to acquire a taste for such initially less pleasurable things as vegetables, salads, and whole wheat bread.

A variation of the pleasure principle is the desire not to displease anybody—an eagerness to please everybody. This is neither possible nor desirable. For example, when an individual or group of individuals is suspected of planning or committing a crime such as burglary or murder, it is the moral duty of a person to report the matter to the police however much he may incur the displeasure of the suspected party by doing so. It does not matter if the suspected party happens to be a very close friend or relative.

Pleasing everybody is not possible either. Whatever a person may decide to do, however just or humanitarian his action may be, he may rest assured of someone's wounded vanity, excited envy, hurt feelings, thwarted purpose. However right and well-meaning his action, he may rest assured that somebody will come along to criticize him. Truth inevitably offends those who practice falsehood. Justice cannot but offend the unjust. The spirit of love provokes those who thrive on hatred. The power of light challenges those who reign in darkness. Even that which appears to be very simple and natural calls forth the adverse comments of those who are sadistic in nature.

There is an ancient story illustrating this truth that nobody can please everybody and that whatever one may do can be the target of criticism. Accompanied by his twelve-year-old son, an elderly man went shopping in a village market about five miles from their home. They purchased some groceries, and a donkey for use in their business. Returning home in the late afternoon, the old man felt pretty tired. So he rode upon the donkey's back and the young boy walked alongside. A group of men saw them from a distance and commented aloud: "Look at that selfish man. He is merrily riding the donkey, compelling the poor little boy to walk along." This remark touched the father to the quick. He decided to walk, and had the boy mount the donkey. No sooner had they gone a little distance than a man shouted out: "What kind of thoughtless and stupid boy are you? You are having a joy ride, compelling your old father to trudge along." On hearing that remark, father and son decided both would share the donkey's back. But they had not gone more than a hundred yards when a pedestrian observed to his companion: "See how those cruel people are driving the poor donkey to death." On hearing this accusatory remark both father and son got down from the donkey's back. They felt pity for the animal. They now decided to walk along with the donkey. But were they then past all criticism? By no means. Another group they passed observed: "Look at those foolish men.

They have a nice, strong donkey. But instead of using it for comfort, they are walking wearily by its side."

The story shows that there can be no line of action which will entirely escape criticism, or which will be pleasing to everybody. In making our decisions, then, we cannot be guided by what "they think" or what "everybody thinks." What everybody thinks is the way of indecision, because it is a mass of self-contradictory opinion. So the basis for decision has to be sought elsewhere.

Another impractical and inadequate principle of decision is that of absolute perfection. Some bright scholars remain barren all their lives because of their commitment to perfection. When they wish to write a book, it must be flawlessly perfect. They withhold their decision to write or express themselves until the glorious moment of perfect creation arrives. So all their lives they pursue the ever-receding goal of perfection. The greater the emphasis upon perfection, the further it recedes. The supreme moment never arrives. So the perfect book is never written. In the same way there are some choosy people who never get married. They aim at the perfect life mate. He or she must fulfill all the requirements of the image of perfection in their minds. But in the actual world such a perfect embodiment is hardly to be met with. So the decision for united living is continuously postponed until all possibility of adjustment between the image and the reality is completely lost.

In the same way there are some fine, idealistic souls who continually postpone their decision for social action until inward perfection or complete God-realization is achieved. In their pursuit of inward perfection they more and more withdraw from society. They justify this withdrawal in the hope of return to society on a perfect basis. But since absolute perfection in any direction is an ever-receding goal, all chances may gradually be lost for the perfectionist to bring himself back to active participation in social evolution.

Closely allied to the principle of perfection is the principle of non-limitation or unrestricted freedom. There are some who regard non-limitation or absolute freedom as the rule of living. They hate to do anything which will in any way limit them. In social affairs they advocate the principle of anarchy. In personal life they emphasize the motto of nonconformity. Submission to any law is curtailment of liberty. Commitment to any specific line of action or any determinate scale of values is a fall from the heaven of boundless possibility. So in accepting the principle of unrestricted freedom, they fail to make any decision in the sphere of action. They prefer to float indecisively upon the sea of endless possibility. Their interminable indecision in actual life is grounded in their fascination for the limitless. In the absence of any determinate action, all possibilities are divested of any chance of actual fulfillment. So the principle of unrestricted freedom eventually drives one into the nothingness of empty imagination.

ESSENTIAL FACTORS IN DECISION-MAKING

We are now in a position to identify the essential factors involved in sound and adequate decision. It may be briefly stated that the self-as-related-to-Being is the most valid ground of all fruitful decision. The essential factors in decision-making are: (a) a comprehensive survey of different possibilities; (b) communion with the self; (c) intelligent selection; (d) acceptance of risk, responsibility, and suffering.

The German philosopher Leibniz says that before the creation of the world, endless possibilities of combination of monads—that is, the spiritual atoms which are the ultimate constituents of the universe—hovered before the mind of God. God contemplated such endless possibilities and selected from them one specific combination as the best of them all. What was His ground of selection? The principle of goodness, which is the essence of His being. That is why the actual world in which we live is the best of all possible worlds, all its inherent deficiencies and imperfections notwithstanding. God's creative energy transformed the selected combination of monads into the realm of actuality.

But what is the principle of goodness that determined God's decision at the moment of creation? The principle of goodness is one with the very self—the inmost essence of God. God is absolute goodness. Divine goodness does not consist in conformity to any external standard or law, because there is no law or standard outside of God. So God's selection or decision is not an arbitrary or whimsical one. But is there any way of further specifying the essence of divine goodness, especially insofar as it functions as the criterion of decision?

Religiously speaking, divine goodness is identical with the spirit of love. God decides out of the fullness of love for all concerned. In the motivation of love, one's deepest delight consists in insuring the maximum welfare of all, individually and collectively. This is so because in love the All of existence is felt as inseparably one with the self. Love is the unity of self-interest and other-interest. It is the indivisible unity of egoism and altruism. From the human standpoint, egoism and altruism are felt as separate impulses, because the self and the other are experienced as discontinuous. This is man's ignorance (*avidyā*). On the basis of ignorance, love appears as the sacrifice of the self for the sake of the other; goodness appears as the restraining of the self in consideration of the other. But from the standpoint of wisdom, the real is the undivided unity of the self and the other. So love is active interest in the cosmic good.

Philosophically speaking, divine goodness is rooted in the ontological structure of God. Divinity is the attribute of the self-as-related-to-Being. So the self-Being (*ātman-Brahman*) is the standard of all good decision. The self does not exist as an isolated, self-absorbed entity. So there is no goodness in the arbitrary decision of a self-absorbed individual. Similarly, there is no Being, no All of existence, apart from the self as the center of action. So goodness cannot result from the abstract consideration of the All of existence or from unthinking conformity to the overwhelming power of Being. Authentic awareness of the self is the awareness of the self-as-related-to-Being. It is the awareness of the identity of the All of existence with the individual self. The spirit of goodness and love flows from such authentic self-awareness and serves as the stable basis for the most fruitful decisions in life.

A bright young boy has just entered college. He is vaguely aware of many talents lying dormant within him. He can become a great poet or a musician if he wants to. He can become a great scientist if he applies himself in that direction. There is no reason why he cannot also become a successful politician or moral reformer or dynamic spiritual leader, and so on and so forth. For some time he becomes intensely interested in

poetry and music and studies whatever relevant books
he can lay his hands upon. But after a while his interest
and enthusiasm in these fields evaporate. He now becomes tremendously interested in religion and philosophy. He spends days and nights in studying and dis-
cussing philosophical and religious issues. But after a
while this interest also evaporates. He now turns his
attention to such subjects as economics and politics. For
a while he is all excited about this new-found interest.
But unfortunately this also does not last very long.
Other neglected things enchant him from a distance.
Our young friend thus goes on floating upon the sea of
endless, fascinating possibilities. He seems incapable of
limiting himself to a well-chosen course. He is enchanted by the limitless.

But indecisive floating among possibilities leaves him
nowhere. It makes him a jack-of-all-trades, but master of
none. It involves a tragic waste of talent. A sense of self-
dissipation and frustration eventually assails his mind.
Even the omnipotent God had to make a selection from
boundless possibilities in order to create. Similarly an
individual, however talented and brilliant, must make
an intelligent selection from the numerous possibilities
of his nature, in order to be successful and fruitful in
life. He has to make a realistic estimate of the various
dynamic potentialities of his nature. On that basis he
has to decide what should be his main career in life—art,
science, statecraft, religion, or social reform. His other
strong interests can be organized around his central
purpose of life as side occupations or hobbies. If for
example he decides to be predominantly a scientist, his
interest in sports or poetry or politics may be retained as
leisure-time pursuits.

Now if he decides to become predominantly a scientist, this decision must flow from his own self. He makes this decision not because of his father or his teacher, but because of his own predominant interest and talent. He feels that it is as a scientist that he can be most true to himself and bring out the best within himself.

But he does not exist only for himself. He belongs to a family, to a community, to a country, to the human race. In the ultimate analysis, he belongs to a cosmic order of things. Whatever decision he makes in life affects other people and is therefore bound to react upon him. It is as related to the cosmic whole that he lives and functions. So his decision to be a scientist must also involve the decision to offer his services as a scientist for the good of humanity. In deciding to develop the best within oneself, one has also to decide to give one's best for the cosmic good, the maximum welfare of all, including himself and others. Thus the spirit of love as the principle of the self-as-related-to-Being becomes the guiding principle of mature decision. In deciding to be a scientist and to serve humanity as a scientist, one has to sacrifice other possibilities. One has to endure hardship and be painstaking. One must expect to encounter criticism and opposition. One has to take risks and assume responsibilities. Squarely faced and boldly accepted, they all contribute to strength of character and nobility of personality. They all contribute to the profound joy of creative self-expression.

Besides such major decisions as those related to marriage, career, social service, or religious commitment, we all have to make many minor decisions in life. New situations constantly arise, calling upon us to make decisions afresh. A long-time friend is secretly thwarting my interests. Should I expose him at the risk of open hostility? A sworn enemy is willing to come to terms. Should I agree to enter into a business transaction with him? In dealing with a dangerous burglar or kidnapper, should I take risk in adopting a nonviolent approach, or should I be ready to kill him if necessary? In dealing with such emergent situations there is no magic formula which can be blindly applied in all circumstances. Every situation has to be carefully considered in its concrete fullness. When time permits, well-wishers and trustworthy authorities can be consulted. But finally a decision has always to be made in the depths of one's own being. The habit of sleeping over a crucial matter or that of retiring into the silence of mature deliberation is an invaluable asset. The ultimate deciding factor should be neither extreme egoism nor abstract altruism. Extreme egoism is self-defeating. Abstract altruism is self-frustrating and self-annihilating. The golden principle of decision in all cases is the self-as-related-to-Being (*ātman-Brahman*). It is active awareness of the self as a component of the cosmic whole and as a creative source of cosmic good. It is awareness of the self as a unique center of action of Being.

CHAPTER VI

The Problem of Suffering

SUFFERING IS UNIVERSALLY FELT as diminution of being. So the natural impulse of all living creatures is to eschew suffering. It is inherent in the pursuit of happiness which is a universal instinct. Pain is experienced as a disvalue, as a negative fact, as the negation of being. Pleasure is the positive goal of all normal endeavors. It is experienced as a plus value, as an essential ingredient of happiness.

An ontological insight into the structure of life reveals that life is the unity of being and nonbeing. It is the indivisible nexus of positive and negative factors. Every living thing comes into existence out of nonbeing, constantly changes while living, and passes into nonbeing again at the end of its life. Even the eternally perfect God has an unmanifest, unfathomable and indeterminable aspect. This is the element of nonbeing in God. God manifests Himself by creating this world out of that original, inexhaustible Nothingness.

If then being and nonbeing inseparably intermingle in the structure of the real, pain and pleasure, suffering and happiness cannot be absolutely separated from each other. Pain prevents pleasure from evaporating. Pleasure prevents pain from disintegrating. Pain gives pleasure a reality basis. Pleasure imparts to pain the dynamics of growth. Pain is confrontation with the power of nonbeing. Pleasure is the expression of the surging power of being.

God who is perfect bliss does also suffer. He suffers in sacrificing His infinitude while creating the world of the finite. He suffers by descending into the heart of darkness in order to create there the kingdom of light. He suffers by fighting with the forces of chaos in creating the historical order.

Man suffers most when he becomes intensely aware of his own limitations. But his profoundest suffering is also the moment of his greatest joy. In the very act of clearly apprehending his limitations, he transcends, in a sense, all limitation. He catches a glimpse of the unlimited that dwells right within himself surrounded by numberless limitations. Thus pain and pleasure become one in his exalted moment of enlightenment.

It follows that the ultimate goal of life is not any utopian pleasure or happiness absolutely free of all pain and suffering. Unmixed pleasure is neither real nor desirable. It is not real insofar as it is unrelated to fact. It fails to take into account the moment of nonbeing in our life. Unmixed pleasure is also not desirable, because it could induce life to squander itself. Pain is an essential ingredient in the creative urges and ever-new birth pangs of life. The ultimate goal of life may be defined as that dynamic happiness which unifies pain and pleasure within itself. In ultimate self-fulfillment there is the joy of union with the Fount of all being. There is also the joy of functioning as an active channel of expression of the glory of Being. But the crown of glory is always made of thorns. In manifesting the glory of Being the assaults of nonbeing have to be endured. The possibility of suffering inflicted by opposition and hostility has to be gladly accepted. The burden of love, the anxiety of action, the pain of participation in world affairs, have to be embraced. In accepting a life of active participation in the world in union with the Supreme Being, there is profound creative joy in which pain and pleasure intermingle.

This may be seen as an integral view of the meaning of suffering. In the history of thought the problem of suffering has often been approached from two extreme angles: the subjectivist and the objectivist. Very few are those who have grasped a balanced approach to the problem. Suffering is not to be discarded as a total disvalue. It has to be integrated into the dynamism of creative joy. It is a spur to fresh effort. It is an integral part of voluntary self-giving for the good of the universe. That is why the Buddha gave up the earthly kingdom and later on even the heavenly kingdom (*Parinirvāna*) with a view to serving all living creation. That is also why Christ contemptuously rejected Satan's offer of sovereignty over the whole world with a view to redeeming mankind. The suffering of self-sacrifice for the sake of cosmic welfare is indeed the very core of mature spiritual joy.

Let us now briefly discuss the extremely subjectivist and the extremely objectivist theories of suffering. That will prepare the ground for a fuller understanding of the integral view of suffering as an essential phenomenon of life which is compounded of being and nonbeing.

THE SUBJECTIVIST VIEW OF SUFFERING

The subjectivist theory traces all human suffering to a subjective cause. In Western theology the root cause of all suffering is the original sin. The original sin committed by Adam and Eve plunged the human race into the abysmal pit of suffering. The original sin is self-originating and self-multiplying. Sin begets sin, and still more sin. Born out of original sin, the descendants of Adam and Eve are caught in the swelling momentum of sin's snowballing. Man is powerless to stop it. God alone can lift man out of his disaster. So He makes a sacrifice and takes suffering upon Himself. He avenges His own wrath and actively reveals the other side of His being—His love and forgiveness. By the power of love, God the Son makes atonement for the original sin on behalf of the human race. Thereafter it is open to any human individual to take advantage of that atonement, an abrogation of sin, by accepting and identifying himself with the atoning, divine personality. Therein lies the one hope of suffering humanity—the only hope of final salvation from the vicious circle of sin and suffering.

In Judaism and Islam the fundamental approach is the same with some doctrinal variations. All suffering does indeed flow ultimately from the original sin. The original sin begets sinful propensities in all humans. Fresh sinful actions further augment and intensify the dark seed of the original sin. The path of salvation lies in rediscovering the divine will and in wholeheartedly accepting the revealed word of God. Every individual has to make this rediscovery and make sufficient penances for his past sins. Islam has cherished the revealed word of God in the Koran. Judaism has preserved the revealed word of God in the Torah. In reorganizing one's whole life on the basis of total submission to the divine will as thus revealed, the attainment of salvation and the kingdom of heaven is assured. The practice of penance and austerity as recommended in the revealed scriptures produces increasing self-purification. The performance of the recommended virtues of faith, prayer, obedience and charity brings on mounting spiritual ascension. The responding grace of God burns up the last vestiges of the sin original. The final gateway to the kingdom of heaven visualized as the land of no suffering is opened.

The orthodox Hindu-Buddhist religious tradition is also subjectivist in outlook. Only the root cause of all suffering is identified here as original ignorance (*avidyā*) instead of original sin. The ignorance from which all suffering ultimately flows is neither intellectual nor empirical. It is not a matter of failure on the part of the intellect to comprehend the fundamental truth. At the beginning the intellect is not even developed as a differentiated faculty of the mind. Nor is the original ignorance empirical in the sense of lack of acquaintance with certain facts about the external world. For example, the original ignorance of a person does not consist in the fact that he is innocent of physics or chemistry or mathematics or history. Nor does it consist of such intellectual incompetence as lack of training in dialectics or symbolical logic. A person may be a living encyclopedia of scientific knowledge, or he may be a master logician, but still he may be in bondage and suffering on account of his original ignorance, that is, his ignorance about his own higher self. Original ignorance consists in the lack of awareness of the essential structure of his own true self. What is the inmost essence of his own being? How is he related to the cosmic whole or to his environment? How is he related to the ultimate ground of existence? It is ignorance about these basic

facts about oneself which is the fundamental cause of
suffering and bondage. Original ignorance is ontological
ignorance.

Since the above view is in essential respects radically
different from the doctrine of original sin, a little elaboration will be in order here.

Let us suppose that a great atomic scientist is in the
employ of an ambitious dictator or military ruler. He
knows that the particular atomic research project upon
which he is engaged is going to be used in fulfilling the
military ambitions of the ruling political power, involving a ruthless massacre of the innocent. He knows that
such military expansionism is an evil, a crime against
humanity. But still he chooses to be an accomplice in
this criminal design. Considerations of personal glory
and prosperity determine his choice. So an evidently
evil course appears as good by reason of personal considerations which present themselves as reasonable excuses
or rationalizations. Having decided to work in com-
plicity with a military dictator, the atomic scientist in
question may now begin to believe sincerely that that is
the right course for him to follow. And therein lies the
core of his original ignorance (*avidyā*). Conscious or
unconscious motivation of an egoistic character, a perverse will which chooses that which is known to be detrimental to cosmic good, a desire for personal aggran-
dizement at the cost of the social welfare—these are all
concrete manifestations of original ignorance.

The essence of original ignorance lies in the false
identification of the self with the ego. The self is a
unique focus of the infinite and a creative center of the
cosmic whole. Awareness of the authentic self can never
allow egotistic motivations to take precedence over
cosmic welfare. Perversity of the will and egotistic pro-

pensities are burnt up in the flaming light of total self-knowledge. It is in the absence of ontological self-awareness that the self is alienated from its true essence and functions as the ego. The ego is a distorted reflection of the authentic self. It is the self oblivious of its ontological root and essential structure. It is the self estranged from its own ground due to original ignorance. A product of self-ignorance, the ego affirms itself in opposition to the cosmic welfare. Such divisions within human personality as intellect and will, knowledge of good and choice of evil, love of truth and addiction to falsehood, flow from the original self-ignorance of the individual. So in the Hindu-Buddhist spiritual tradition, original ignorance is identified as the root cause of all human suffering. Egoism (*asmitā*) and selfish desire (*tanhā* or *kāma*), the predominance of personal likes and dislikes, love and hatred (*rāga-dveṣa*), subjectively colored conceptions of good and evil (*dvandva*), are the various offspring of the original ignorance.

We have seen that in the Western religious tradition, salvation lies in emancipation from original sin. Such an emancipation is provided by total acceptance of, and conformity to, the divine will as revealed in the scriptures. In the Hindu-Buddhist religious tradition, salvation lies in liberation from the bonds of original ignorance. Now the best way to dispel the darkness of ignorance is to kindle the light of total insight into the heart of Being. So liberation consists in total illumination or luminous union with the authentic self or the ground of existence. It has been variously called *prajñā, bodhi, satori, samādhi, jñāna,* etc. It is the ontological insight born of the complete integration of personality. Scripture, ethical action, self-discipline, religious observances, are only aids to that ultimate enlightenment which alone can dispel the original ignorance. Enlightenment is not mere faith, but personal realization of the truth. Faith is further transformed here into living, flaming experience—the experience of the individual's total union with the cosmic reality.

THE OBJECTIVIST APPROACH

In all countries and in all ages, besides the religious and mystical tradition, there is also the secular and socio-political tradition. While the religious tradition is predominantly subjectivistic, the socio-political tradition is predominantly objectivistic in its outlook. Whereas the former is predominantly introverted, the latter is predominantly extroverted.

According to the objectivist approach, human suffering is the result of unfavorable external circumstances. The more man succeeds in intelligently changing outward circumstances of living, the more he can eliminate suffering from life. The chief causes of human suffering are poverty, illiteracy, social inequality, political subjugation, overpopulation, and natural catastrophies like famine, earthquake, volcanic eruptions, and floods.

In tackling the aforesaid causes of suffering, suitable changes have to be made in the socio-political structure. Inequalities must be removed from the social fabric so that all individuals—born equal—may be provided with equal opportunity for growth and social participation. There should be suitable institutions for an equitable distribution of national wealth among all people. A nation, being essentially indivisible, cannot be half-free and half-slave or half-fed and half-starved. The political structure of the nation should be such that this indivisibility is taken into full account.

Just as a nation cannot live half-free and half-slave, similarly the international community cannot for long be half-free and half-slave, half-prosperous and half-poor. So long as vast international inequalities continue to exist in the form of colonialistic exploitation and political domination of one country over another, the agonies of human suffering are bound to rend the skies. So there is a paramount need for such international institutions as the UN, UNESCO, World Health Organization, and World Bank as agencies for international harmony, progress, and peace.

There are three big problems which beset the objectivist formula for human happiness. First, there is the problem of ideology. After it is admitted that the key to the problem of suffering is an ideal change of socio-economic-political circumstances, mutually conflicting theories about the precise nature of such desirable change may become rampant. In the name of human happiness and world peace, antagonistic ideologies may threaten to shatter world peace. They may hang like the sword of Damocles over the international community. Some enthusiastic champions of a worldly kingdom of heaven may even dream of building their kingdom over the atomic ruins of the entire civilization.

Secondly, there is the problem of the human factor. This is inseparably connected with the first problem. However perfect the institutions and organized structures of a society may be, in ultimate analysis it is the human factor which counts most. It is the character of the man behind the machine which counts most. It is the inner nature, the purpose and motivation of the individuals operating the social institutions, upon which the real well-being of the people ultimately depends. A perfect machine without a dedicated soul behind it may prove dangerously deceptive. A community may be equipped with ideal democratic institutions and magnificent welfare projects, but still in the absence of a fairly good measure of public intelligence and communal integrity, corruption and class exploitation may become rampant. The entire community may unwittingly become a pawn in the power drive of an ambitious clique. So the issue of social welfare and human happiness cannot, after all, be separated from the subjective factor, namely the question of the level of intelligence and the moral integrity of the people and of the powers that be.

The third problem lies in the destructiveness of the path of desire. Those who pin their faith upon the favorable change of environment as the sole answer to man's search for happiness, conceive of happiness as the fulfillment of desire. Suffering is the frustration of desire. Man suffers when he lacks opportunities for the fulfillment of his various desires. Good opportunities for adequate training and education are an important step in the quest for happiness. Respectable social position and a comfortable job are essential for happiness. Satisfactory marriage and a circle of trustworthy friends can immensely contribute to solid and abiding happiness. Various labor-saving devices and convenient gadgets further enhance happiness. Technological mastery over the forces of nature can enormously increase and diversify happiness. But the question arises: After a man has procured all these external means and outward conditions of happiness, can he still be assured of genuine happiness? Is happiness really a product of the fulfillment of desire?

Experience shows that our desires have a knack of multiplying themselves. As soon as a particular set of

desires is satisfied, a fresh crop of desires looms large on
the horizon. And there seems to be no end to the mush-
rooming of the ever-new desires. The more we add fuel
to the fire, the more the flame goes up. Similarly, the
more we procure various objects of desire, the more the
flame of desire keeps roaring, until perhaps not even
the whole world can satisfy it. Incapable of being satisfied, it turns upon itself and consumes its own base and
ground. Thus unrestrained desire proves destructive. A
person who follows the path of desire eventually perishes. Death dwells in the heart of desire. Or, it may be
said that death and desire are two faces of the same
demon. In Hindu-Buddhist psychology this demon is
known as *Kāma-Māra* (Desire-Death). Modern psycho-
analysis has rediscovered this truth in a different form.
Sigmund Freud has identified the two fundamental
instinctual drives of human personality as life instinct
(eros) and death instinct (thanatos). These two instincts are inseparably intertwined. If there is any abiding and supreme happiness within the range of human
possibility, it must be conditional upon the discovery of
some truth or reality beyond the desire-death polarity,
beyond eros-thanatos or *Kāma-Māra*.

An ancient story poignantly illustrates the destructiveness of mere desire. An ambitious man was on the
lookout for some hidden treasure or magic formula for
prosperity and happiness. Searching far and wide, he
came to meet a great sage in a Himalayan cave. He
prayed to the sage for some tangible token of his blessing. At his repeated request, the sage gave him a magic
seat. When a person after taking a bath and putting on
clean clothes sits upon this seat and makes a wish, it is
immediately granted. All excited in joy, the man hurried home with the magic seat. After scrupulously ful-

filling the conditions of cleanliness, he took his seat and wished for a sumptuous dinner. Immediately he was served with dainty dishes and he ate to his heart's content. Then a snowballing mass of desires surged up wildly and ran riot in his heart. He wished for a magnificent palace for his residence. He wished for the palace to be most tastefully decorated and furnished with the most modern articles of furniture. He wished for a beautiful young wife. He wished to have several servants ever ready to cater to his needs and comforts. He rubbed his eyes with utter astonishment to see his procession of fancy desires fulfilled to perfection one after another. But in the midst of all this wondrous wish-fulfillment, he was suddenly horrified to behold within himself a lurking desire to die. Or, was it fear of death, a shudder at the prospect of suffocation in the meshes of desire? The thought arose in his mind: What if, at night, a band of cruel robbers entered my palace and helped themselves to all these new-found treasures by dealing me a death blow? No sooner had the thought arisen than the stage was set for the tragic disaster. In the midst of his freshly acquired abundance and luxury, he experienced the shattering power of nothingness. The moment of unrestricted wish-fulfillment merged into the moment of irrevocable annihilation.

It is because desire holds within itself the seed of death that extraordinarily successful people are often known to collapse at the very height of success. The sun begins to decline immediately after reaching the zenith. Immediately after hitting the long-desired million mark, a millionaire often is assailed by the panic of inner emptiness. He may be unable to think of anything else except embracing sweet death. The saturation point of desire is inwardly devastating. The policy of unrestricted wish-fulfillment is sure to beget a plethora of mutually conflicting wishes. Selection of some wishes naturally drives others into suppression. The satisfaction of the chosen desires is the occasion for the suppressed desires to wreak vengeance.

The path of desire is then not the way to conquer suffering. By creating ever-new opportunities for wish-fulfillment, one cannot insure ultimate happiness. Is it then the policy of absolute desirelessness that provides the answer to the problem of suffering? The religious tradition of the past has been inclined on the whole to say "yes" to this question. Desire that holds the seed of death is the root cause of suffering. Natural impulses and desires of the human mind have been condemned by traditional religious beliefs as evil. Sex has been identified as the arch enemy of the religiously and mystically minded people. A radical antagonism has been imagined to exist between the flesh and the spirit, between the natural and the supernatural, between the empirical and the transcendental. So in the Western religious tradition ultimate happiness has been associated with a supernatural kingdom of heaven. This supernatural realm of happiness can be achieved either after death by virtue of other-worldly religiosity, or it may perhaps be built on earth out of the ruins of the natural order by virtue of nontemporal piety. In the Eastern religious tradition, the sphere of supreme happiness has been identified with the nontemporal dimension of existence which is capable of being realized here and now through man's mystic union with the infinite. But the *sine qua non* of such mystic experience is complete desirelessness, a total liquidation of all natural impulses.

THE INTEGRAL APPROACH

The objectivist formula cannot solve the problem of suffering because uncontrolled desire is death-dealing. It is the serpent that bites the hand that feeds him. The subjectivist formula tries to solve the problem by providing an escape from suffering. It encourages the negative approach of suppressing or withdrawing from the life of desire. It fosters other-worldliness either of the supernatural order (as in the West) or of the nontemporal order (as in the East). But in following this negative policy of escapism, however much a few individuals may gain in terms of blissful religious experience on a certain level of personality, the amount of suffering in the world goes on increasing instead of diminishing. The imperative need for the betterment of the material conditions of living in this world is neglected. Even the few individuals who succeed in attaining blissful religious or mystical experience suffer immensely on the physical plane on account of poverty, disease, malnutrition, premature death. There is absolutely no reason to consider such suffering as an inescapable concomitant of religious growth. To try to conquer suffering by withdrawing from the life of desire is like discarding the rose for its thorns.

Desire is no doubt a driving force of life. But it is neither good nor evil. It is ethically neutral. It is the fundamental energy of life; it is limitless potentiality. It is neither ignorance nor knowledge. It is a grievous error to consider desire either an unmitigated evil or a product of absolute ignorance.

Positively speaking, desire is both good and evil. Desire in its extremely selfish and egotistic form is an evil.

But desire in its altruistic form, desire as longing for higher values, desire as passion for good, is good. Such altruistic desire is as natural as egotistic desire. Egotistic desire is ignorant, because the individual is unreal except as an integral member of the cosmic whole. But when desire assumes the form of dedication to collective good or cosmic welfare, it becomes a function of knowledge.

It is true that there is a trace of ignorance (*avidyā*) even in altruistic and humanitarian desires or in cultural and spiritual striving, so long as the individual has not realized the eternal, the nontemporal dimension of existence. This is so because the individual has no reality except as a mode of expression of the eternal. Rootedness in the supracosmic eternal is the ultimate essence of his being. Direct awareness of this supraconscious or nontemporal essence involves a radical transformation of all desire. But what the light of supreme wisdom requires is the enlightening and transforming of desire, not its annihilation. If the life of an individual has an ultimate meaning, desire which is of the essence of individual existence must also have an ultimate meaning.

The meaning of desire lies in the purpose of creating ever-new values. That is the original and ultimate purpose of creation itself. Desire in its spiritual essence is the urge of creative self-expression. When extreme selfishness and egotism obstruct the functioning of desire as a means of manifesting the glory of being, they betray themselves as ignorance and evil. When the vision of such higher values as truth, beauty, freedom, love, progress, turns desire into creative energy, it functions as a dynamic force of knowledge. The key to the problem of suffering is to be found in the increasing transformation of desire. Neither the pampering nor the destroying of desire—neither the multiplication nor the liquidation of desire—can solve the problem.

The ultimate goal of man is neither a compromise with suffering nor an escape from suffering. It is not self-delusion through endless multiplication of desires as is done in a positively materialistic program of life. Nor is it self-annihilation through the uprooting of all desires as is done in a negatively spiritualistic program of life. The ultimate goal of man is the conquest of suffering on the basis of complete self-affirmation in union with the eternal.

FOURFOLD HAPPINESS

Happiness, which is the object of all human endeavor, involves fourfold joy: natural, transcendental, creative, and dialectic. Natural joy consists just in existing, in breathing the breath of life, in enduring as an integral part of the natural order. There is joy in waking up in the morning and in looking at the glorious sunrise. There is joy in bathing in a stream, with the silent approval of surrounding trees and to the accompaniment of the singing birds. There is a joy in being hungry and in satisfying hunger with a delicious meal. There is joy in getting thirsty and in satisfying thirst with a glass of pure water. There is joy in making friends, in sharing with them the delights of life, and also once in a while in quarreling with them. Life with all its tears and laughter is indeed in ultimate analysis an expression of very deep joy.

The transcendental joy is the joy of immediate existential contact with the eternal, or the nontemporal dimension of Being. It is the joy of *nirvāna, samādhi,* or unitive consciousness. It is what Sri Aurobindo has called the "eternal and immutable delight of being."* The Upaniṣads declare that when the eternal is envisioned, all bonds of attachment are snapped, all doubts are dissolved, all sins are washed away.** The last lingering traces of fear and anxiety, of guilt and inferiority, melt away. The entire personality is inundated with that unspeakable joy which flows profusely from the Fount of all being. The transcendental joy is the joy that dwells in the element of pure transcendence in human existence.

But the nontemporal is inseparable from the creative. Being is inseparable from becoming. Śiva is inseparable from Śakti. The two are different dimensions of the same indivisible Being. So total self-affirmation implies affirming the creative as well as the nontemporal, the dynamic as well as the static aspects of Being. The affirmation of the creative aspect of Being is the root of creative joy. It is the joy of mutable becoming. It is the joy of accepting the world as the medium in which the glory of Being is to be manifested. It is the joy of accepting the material and social environment as the medium in which the splendors of pure transcendence are to be given concrete embodiment. It is the joy of accepting the realm of darkness as the sphere in which the infinite light is to be expressed in endless colors. In adopting this affirmative attitude there is the sorrow of self-limitation, the pain of sacrifice, the anxiety about the power of darkness and nonbeing, the fear of hostility and opposition. Creative joy takes this negative element upon itself, and thus transforms it into its own intensities. Suffering is accepted as a subdued element in the struc-

* Sri Aurobindo, *The Life Divine* (Pondicherry: Sri Aurobindo Ashram, 1955), p. 123.
** Mundaka Upaniṣad, II, 2.9.

ture of creative joy. Especially for an individual who has experienced the transcendental joy of the eternal, the pain of creative self-affirmation can never prove upsetting or paralyzing. Even dismal failure and frustration can be gratefully accepted as part of the game of life—of *līlā,* of existence as divine drama.

Fourthly, there is the dialectical joy. It is the joy of surmounting obstacles and conquering opposition. In affirming the world as the medium of creative self-expression, an encounter with the forces of ignorance and inertia, with the forces of darkness and evil, is only to be expected. There is joy in accepting the challenge of opposition. Even if one meets with failure and defeat in a brave and honest confrontation with the forces of opposition, there is a glory in such defeat. But if one meets with success, there is double joy in one's victory. The joy of squarely facing opposition, or overcoming resistance, is the dialectical joy. All suffering incidental to such an heroic approach is transmuted into an element of the overruling harmony of dialectical joy.

The fourfold joy as the positive goal of life is the final answer to the problem of human suffering.

CHAPTER VII

Wisdom in Human Relations

WISDOM IN HUMAN RELATIONS is the mark of a mature personality. It is conducive to happiness in life and also to spiritual growth. It is essential for personal success as well as for social welfare and advancement.

In building up a successful career, what a person knows, what his equipment and training is, is not enough. Who are the persons he knows—this counts a good deal. The ability to make right contacts and to turn them into an asset is of capital importance. Success is not simply a question of how much skill one has, but of how well he can get along with others. Many brilliant artists, scholars, and technicians have been failures in society because of arrogance, pride, lack of personal charm and warmth. On the other hand, people with much less talent but endowed with humility, reliability, loyalty and cooperativeness, are known to have attained enormous success.

That the strength and development of a nation or organization should depend upon right human relations is quite obvious. The more it succeeds in presenting a united front to the outside world, the stronger its position, the greater the respect and admiration it can command. A sense of solidarity and a spirit of cooperation among its members are the *sine qua non* of inward strength and steady progress.

But even in the process of spiritual fulfillment and constructive self-development of an individual, human relations play a very dominant role. This is so because relations enter into the essential structure of the individual self. Apart from relations to the social environment, the individual self is a mere abstraction. The individual who lives in the forest away from society is either a beast or an angel, as Aristotle observed. It may be added that even an angel can function true to his essence only in an appropriate social medium. Torn away from the relations of love and good action, even an angel would be degraded beyond all recognition.

Relations are essential to the growth of the individual soul, because the individual in his essence is not an isolated entity. He is not like a Lucretian atom, solid in singleness and enclosed within itself. He exists in close interdependence and interrelationship with his fellow beings. He grows through constant social intercourse with others. He belongs inseparably to a community and a country. He belongs in a larger perspective to the international human family. From a still broader standpoint, he belongs to the cosmic whole, to the entire universe. Relatedness to the social context or cosmic whole is then an essential ingredient of the individual. So the development of an individual as an individual requires increasing skill in the adjustment of his relations to others. It consists in joining hands with others in constructive cooperation without loss of inner freedom and sense of value.

The ultimate goal of human life is essentially connected with the concept of human relations. In medieval times the spiritual destiny of life was conceived of more or less negatively as liberation from all bonds of relationship. It was believed that since the individual springs into existence out of the absolute, his ultimate goal is to return to either supernatural or transcendental union with the absolute. It was further believed that relatedness in the sphere of the finite is a mode of bondage. Human relations, it was therefore felt, are fetters to be broken in the search for pure transcendence. But a critical examination of the history of the Middle Ages discloses the inadequacy and one-sidedness of that approach. To return to lonely union with the infinite from which the individual came into being is like going back to the point of departure without any gain or achievement. This idea robs life of all purpose and significance. Properly understood, it is not without purpose that individuals become differentiated from the creative universal and enter into all manner of relationships with one another. Part of that purpose is obviously the infinite diversification of the One. It is the self-imaging or self-representation of the One in the individualized Many. It is the growing manifestation of the creative joy of self-differentiation that throbs in the heart of reality. Individuals are increasingly differentiated in order to function as channels of expression of the unlimited glory of the infinite.

So the purpose of individual existence is not to return but to express, not merely to transcend but to create, not to complete a pointless circle but to initiate ever-new circles of form and value. The ability to express oneself autonomously and creatively is of the essence of freedom. It is in the sphere of manifold relations that such freedom can be exercised. So the purpose of life is not freedom *from* relations but freedom *in and through* manifold relations. It is in the midst of a thousand and one social bonds—the bonds of love and action—that dynamic freedom can be enjoyed.

Different people grow up with different emotional attitudes toward the social environment. Such emotional attitudes unconsciously determine their relations with fellow beings. And such relations shape and mold their character. They determine their happiness and mode of self-fulfillment in this world.

ARE ALL MEN GOOD?

Some people grow up with the naïve idea that all individuals are good. They have had no acquaintance with the incredible ugliness of the wicked. They are innocent of the abysmal terrors of evil. Their minds wear colored glasses through which to look at the outside world. Holiness is equated with a pious wish to shut one's eyes to evil, to close one's ears to evil, and to seal one's lips with regard to evil. The evil is believed to be an illusion of the mind. Naturally, therefore, as they come in direct contact with the harsh realities of life, every now and then they become emotionally upset. They may be shocked to the point of nervous breakdown by the selfish betrayal of a friend, or the wanton cruelty of a stranger, or the savage ruthlessness of an enemy. In the absence of a balanced perspective, such shocks prove shattering to a naïve person. He may suffer mental paralysis, withdraw from all social contacts, and decide to live in an imaginary paradise of his own. Thus naïveté in human relations may pave the way to schizophrenia.

The naïve belief that all men are good is essentially different from the spiritual understanding that all men are basically or potentially good. The former implies that all men are good in their social actuality. This is evidently wrong. There are people with incredible depths of wickedness, savagery, and criminality. There are people who can kill women and children just out of an unconscious, compelling urge or for the sake of a neurotic kick. There are men who can cold-bloodedly murder millions of innocent people for the sake of self-glorification. Those who are naïve in human relations become easy victims of such mischief-mongers. They make the mistake of considering childish innocence as a great virtue. Authentic virtue must be broadbased upon a full understanding of the ways of the world, including its perversities as well as nobilities.

The spiritual understanding that all men are in spiritual essence good is based upon full acquaintance with the dismal perversities of human nature. There are people who can be more brutal than beasts. But still there is a silver lining to the darkest clouds of human wickedness. However brutal and criminal a person in his social actuality may be, even he need not be given up as totally lost. Even in him the spiritual potentiality is there, the divine spark is there, the possibility of a radical change is there, an opening to the light and power of higher consciousness is there. It is this spiritual potentiality of man as man which has been at the source of many miraculous religious conversions in history—conversions of the worst sinners into great saints.

So spiritual understanding holds forth the hope of redemption for all, including the worst sinner. It involves compassion for all without having to shut one's eyes to the actual perversions and brutalities of human nature. If necessary, it may also recommend the swift punishment for antisocial forces or a decisive blow against the conspiracy of reactionary elements for the ultimate good of human society. This is what the Bhagavad-Gītā has emphasized. Within a particular society, judicious employment of force in promoting social welfare is not inconsistent with the recognition of the spiritual dignity of all individuals. When compassion tolerates the perversity of individuals who inflict permanent damage upon society, it degenerates into vain sentimentalism. The individual, with all his rights and claims, is in ultimate analysis a unit of the evolutionary world-spirit. When he proceeds to abuse his individual rights in obstructing higher evolution, society has a right to put him in his place and overcome his obstructionism.

ARE ALL MEN EVIL?

Some individuals, on the other hand, grow up with the idea that all men are evil, all cruel, ruthless, and aggressive. They are like hungry wolves out to exploit and eager to devour. So people have to be either kept at a safe distance or propitiated through meek submission. Those who follow the policy of avoidance eventually withdraw into their own private world. Those who follow the policy of appeasement allow themselves to be exploited, dominated, pushed around, or even tortured by others.

Bitter experiences in childhood contribute to the inner conviction that all people are evil, self-seeking, domineering and relentless. Lack of experience of true love and kindness incapacitates some growing children for understanding the reality of kindness and love. They may be driven to the extreme attitude of paranoia. They may see enmity and hostility everywhere. They may live in constant fear of the conspiracy of dark forces against them, and feel helpless against such conspiracy, or they may be inclined to practice all manner of black magic against the ubiquitous enemy.

Naïve faith in the goodness of all people entails a good deal of suffering at the hands of others. It makes one ready to be cheated and exploited. At the other extreme, the universal mistrust of all people entails a good deal of suffering in the shape of isolation and spiritual suffocation. It opens the road of increasing loneliness and alienation from society. The truth of the matter is that sweeping generalizations can be very harmful. It takes all sorts to make this world. Just as there are people who are incredibly wicked and heartless, there are also people who are genuinely good, loving, and kind-hearted. There are people who practice falsehood just for the sake of falsehood; they are identified with the spirit of falsehood. And there are people who tread the path of virtue for the sake of virtue (they are identified with the spirit of virtue). Similarly there are people who worship falsehood in the name of truth, or worship truth in the garb of falsehood.

ARE THERE GOOD GUYS AND BAD GUYS?

Some individuals grow up with a fixed distinction in the mind between good guys and bad guys. Their attitude to the world reflects a deep-seated dichotomy. They dualistically think of the world in terms of black and white, the devil and the divine. They ignore the innumerable shades of color that exist between black and white. They also ignore the fact that good and bad are neither absolute values nor permanently fixed labels. A person who is a good husband and a good father may be a bad officer in relation to his subordinates in the office, and vice versa. A person who is good as a lover of humanity may be considered bad by the members of his community or political party. A person who is considered a dangerous revolutionary, political or religious, may be worshipped as a savior by the masses of the people whose cause he champions. So good and bad are relative terms; they can hardly be used as fixed labels. A person who is considered bad because he is your sole enemy today, may turn into a good friend tomorrow. This may happen by virtue of a change of circumstances, by the prompting of his self-interest, or by way of your own dealings with him. An understanding of the relativity and changeability of such labels as good and bad, friend and foe, is a factor of paramount importance in social adjustment and successful achievement. In individual life this black-and-white logic makes a person a dangerous fanatic. The application of this dichotomy to the international sphere may generate a war hysteria. It may create a climate suitable for internecine warfare, each camp feeling morally justified in destroying the other, even at the risk of its own life.

ARE PEOPLE OBJECTS OR SUBJECTS?

Many individuals grow up with the idea that other people are means to the fulfillment of their own personal ends. They are objects to be used, things to be manipulated, resources to be exploited. Fellow beings are looked upon either as hindrances to the accomplishment of one's own personal goals, or as opportunities in the ways of self-expansion. Such an attitude toward fellow beings may for some time work brilliantly. It may help in attaining meteoric success as a business tycoon or master politician. It may help in gaining fabulous prosperity or sudden popularity. But in the end the soap bubble glittering in the sunshine is likely to burst. Self-aggrandizement based upon social exploitation is an ephemeral thing. To treat a fellow being as a mere means, is to disregard his intrinsic value as an end unto himself. To look upon other individuals as so much material to be exploited, is to violate the sanctity of society as a spiritual commonwealth. Such a violation is sure to recoil upon oneself, sooner or later. That is why the person who lives by the sword eventually perishes by the sword. The person who prospers through ruthless exploitation one day finds his own soul dead through suffocation. He experiences the horror of nothingness within himself. No amount of accumulated riches can cover up the inward emptiness.

BIPOLARITY OF THE INDIVIDUAL

The ontological insight which forms the core of wisdom in human relations affirms the essential bipolarity of every individual. Every human being is both a means and an end. He is at once a body and a soul, a subject and an object, a spiritual entity and a mass of energy. As a spiritual entity he is a value unto himself, he has a meaningful purpose or destiny of his own life, he is a subject. As an objective means he is instrumental to the advancement of society and the growth of civilization. Intelligent awareness of this instrumental character lies at the root of a person's voluntary self-sacrifice at the altar of the collective good of society. In spiritual enlightenment an individual's dual characteristic of means and end, of body and soul, is unified. The more a person realizes his own soul, the more his vision of cosmic good is made clear and dynamic. The more a person participates in the unfoldment of cosmic welfare, the more his individual life becomes meaningful and fruitful. In serving a supra-individual purpose, he attains the highest glory of his own individuality.

HINDRANCES TO
HARMONIOUS HUMAN RELATIONSHIP

There are certain roadblocks to right relationship which frequently mess up our relations with other people. Among them are: intolerance, possessiveness, hypersensitivity, moralism, and mammonism.

The spirit of intolerance is born of an "I know it all" attitude. It is the offspring of dogmatism. Possessiveness is the tendency to treat one's love object as one's private property. Hypersensitivity is the failure to have an objective understanding of other people on account of morbid preoccupation with one's subjective feelings. Moralism is overemphasis upon abstract moral principles without due consideration for human limitations and human welfare. Mammonism is the pursuit of money as the chief good of life at the sacrifice of humanistic and spiritual values. It looks upon human beings as so many money-making machines.

There are people who are rigidly dogmatic in their views. What they consider to be right is absolutely right. Those who disagree must be stupid or misled by the devil. This intolerant attitude is a huge roadblock to the constructive joining of hands in the pursuit of a common goal. The intolerant ones try desperately to impose their views forcibly upon others, or to reject or destroy those who insist on their right to disagree. But both forcible conversion and violent rejection are detrimental to a healthy build-up of human relations. It is natural for people to have different views. And different views may represent different perspectives of the same multiform reality. An agreement to disagree is the first important step toward human cooperation. Once the right to disagree is accepted, the need to sink differences in cooperative endeavor directed toward a common goal begins to be appreciated. There can be no abiding love between two individuals except on the basis of acceptance of differences. This is true with regard to father and son, brother and brother, husband and wife, neighbor and neighbor. If the differences characteristic of two individuals, however close to each other, are violently suppressed or callously disregarded, great damage is inflicted upon their mutual relationship. When such differences are frankly acknowledged and incorporated into a plan of cooperative co-existence, individuals can vitally stimulate and vastly enrich each other.

EMOTIONAL IMMATURITY

The most baffling impediment to the deepening of love is emotional immaturity. It consists of the inability to survive the weather changes of love. Love as a human relationship has its four seasons of spring, summer, autumn, and winter. Spring is the honeymoon period. Summer is the period of fulfillment. Autumn is the period of decline, the period of growing misunderstanding and disenchantment. Winter is the period of mounting resentment and mutual recrimination. When love survives all these seasonal changes, it discovers a solid core of stability. When two individuals discover that they have the same purposes in life, that they have an abiding interest in the welfare of each other, and that they can sink their differences for the sake of their common cause, then no unfavorable wind can tear up their relationship.

During the springtime of love there is mutual enchantment. There is an upsurge of the positive forces of love. All differences and disconcerting features are thrown into the background or driven underground. A sort of hypnotic spell is created. The elemental urges, the fundamental psychic needs to love and be loved, assert themselves in an overwhelming measure. During the summer of love the newly found relationship reaches its climax and fulfillment. Partners bask in the sunshine of the love that has been realized, in the warmth of the actualized dream.

But then comes the autumn, when the spell begins to wear off and the process of disenchantment sets in. The clay feet of the idol of love are laid bare. The shadow side of personality begins to draw attention. The drawbacks and shortcomings which were submerged in the high tide of mutual admiration show up. The leaves of mutual attraction start falling. Immature love falls therewith.

An immature lover needs a perfect idol, a god, as an object of love. The exuberance of his love impulse can easily deify a suitable person, concealing feet of clay. As soon as the clay feet are revealed, the impulse evaporates and utter frustration follows. But when there is an irrepressible fund of psychic energy, it may proceed to create other god-like idols, one after another, each one to be demolished in due time. Under such conditions love can never strike deep roots.

It is emotional immaturity which gives force to the lure of novelty. An immature love relationship lasts so long as the feeling of novelty endures. With the sense of novelty worn out, love declines. The craving for novelty quickly responds to a new attraction. But it does not take long for the new love to be relegated to the limbo of oblivion. A person who is guided in his choice of friends by the lure of novelty or the glamor of perfection ends up being all alone and lovelorn. Even if he may not mean to reject old friends, friends naturally reject him sooner or later. Friendship is not a thing to be acquired and then taken for granted. It is rather like a living plant that has to be watered regularly, or a flame that has to be fed to keep it burning.

Emotional immaturity engenders hypersensitivity. It does not understand that every human being has his own problems, his own changing moods, his area of privacy, the sanctity of which must be respected. When a person is in a disturbed mood or is preoccupied with an emergent situation, he may naturally fail to respond in his usual manner or with his characteristic warmth and attention to the call of a friend. But if that friend happened to be hypersensitive, he would be quick to jump to conclusions. He would perhaps misconstrue the situation in terms of withdrawal of love. He might even impulsively react with anger and withdrawal on the basis of his hasty conclusion without any attempt to investigate and understand the specific circumstances of the situation.

Immaturity has no grasp of the essence of love as a relationship between two spiritual beings. Consequently it injects into human relations either the instinct of possessiveness and domination, or the policy of appeasement and overindulgence. When an immature person bestows his love upon another individual, he begins to feel that his love is a precious gift to which a high price tag has to be attached. He becomes demanding and exacting. He begins to expect more and more. The gift of his love is believed to confer upon him a property title. He wants to treat his love object as his private property or as a sphere of his sovereign control. He can brook no privacy or area of independence on the part of the person he loves. When love assumes this form, the winter season sets in upon one's emotional life. It heralds the beginning of mutual resentment and recrimination. The weaker party begins to feel suffocated under the tyranny of love. He gets ready to free himself from the golden yoke. He cannot tolerate any longer the profanation of his inner being.

In the contrary case, immaturity represents love as total appeasement. It is believed that in order to love, one must allow the beloved to do as he pleases. To please the object of love by all means becomes the sole concern of the lover. It is such immature love that creates the overindulgent lover. It creates the oversubmissive and mutely suffering wife. It also creates the politician who follows the policy of appeasement in the hope of making friends all around. He sacrifices principle to unreasonable demands. But in the long run such a policy does not pay. The overindulgent mother ruins the future of her child. The oversubmissive wife degrades her husband. The overappeasing politician encourages his enemy to turn into an insatiable tyrant. And eventually the relationship is degraded, if not destroyed.

During the winter season of love, the cold drafts of immature relationship begin to blow freely. The hate component of love comes to the front. Hitherto concealed drawbacks of the partners begin to loom large. Little lapses are magnified beyond proportion. Small unpleasant incidents become occasions for bitter argument and bickering. Tempest-in-a-teapot situations multiply. Mutual recriminations rise in a crescendo.

When the only bond between two partners is a passing advantage or an impulsive infatuation or a legal contract, the rigors of winter can indeed deal the decisive death blow. But when the bond of relationship lies deeper, it may emerge out of the winter ordeal stronger and more stable. A clear understanding of the ultimate purpose of life and devotion to basic principles can stabilize love on a solid foundation. It is the spirit of love as free and joyful self-giving that can unite individuals on a permanent basis.

There can be no abiding human relationship without the warmth of heart and genuine concern for each other. Love can exist without law, because it has a law of its own. As it grows it creates law and order. But divorced from love, law is a hollow thing. It smothers the spirit and turns life into a desert. So a too-legalistic attitude, for all its good intentions, is damaging to human relations. A moralist who is overenthusiastic in his devotion to abstract moral principles is neither effective in his reform nor helpful in his services. People expect from friends, first and foremost, not sermons but sympathy and love. In the absence of sympathy, sermons become repulsive. In the absence of love, ethical pronouncements sound like meaningless platitudes. They are too abstract and general and in consequence out of joint with the specific circumstances and problems that exist in a given situation. Love alone furnishes an insight into the specific nature of human situations. Love with its sympathetic understanding turns righteous indignation into gracious forgiveness. A self-righteous person likes to lift his voice in protest and criticism whenever he sees a flaw in human behavior or a falsehood in social life. He criticizes without any willingness to suffer and sacrifice. He is eager to reform without any understanding of the limitations of human nature. He fails to reform because he forgets to reform himself first. He loses more and more friends, turns friends into enemies, and finds himself impotent in the wilderness. The growing bitterness in his soul is reflected in the harshness of his judgment, and that harshness recoils upon him with ironic fury.

GUIDING PRINCIPLES OF HUMAN RELATIONS

Having discussed some of the roadblocks to satisfactory human relationships, we are now in a position to consider briefly some guiding principles. There are four such principles: (1) delayed response; (2) spirit of accommodation; (3) non-acceptance of unnecessary gifts; (4) tactical toughness.

Many of the blunders we commit in dealing with people are due to the habit of immediate and impulsive reactions. Having acted impulsively, we often regret later on and suffer irrevocably for spoiling a good relationship. You meet an impressive personality to whom you feel attracted. You are emotionally carried off to such an extent that you promptly concede to a request he makes without much thought, or make a promise or commitment, or confide to him a secret about yourself or a common friend. It is too late when you realize that you made a mistake. As you take steps to rectify the situation, you break your relationship with the person. If, however, you decide not to do anything about it, he spoils the relationship by making improper use of the secret you confided, or by taking undue advantage of the promise or commitment you made. In either case, irreparable damage has been done.

So there is a great need to tutor our unconscious

minds not to behave impulsively and emotionally. The principle of delayed response is a useful one. When a critical decision is to be made, it is good to be able to think things over. It is in a cooler moment, when judgment is not swayed by impulse or emotion, that the right decision can be made. When confronted with an unexpected request or demand, it is good to be able to look at the matter from the distance of time instead of making a commitment right then and there. When involved in a provocative situation, it is wise not to respond instantly—and temperamentally. By losing his temper a person always weakens his own case and walks right into the trap of the enemy. Or perhaps he misconstrues the well-meaning criticism of a genuine friend and foolishly injures a beautiful friendship. In order to avoid such tragedies in human relationship, it is desirable to form the habit of delayed response. In dealing with people—friend, foe, or stranger—love and understanding have to be guided by reason so that impulse and emotion may not get the upper hand. Regular practice of meditation is a great help in such self-training. Meditation is the art of harmonizing the unconscious and the conscious. Through meditation, impulse and emotion are brought more and more into harmony with reason. And reason begins more and more to appreciate the importance of different impulses and emotions.

The spirit of accommodation is another guiding principle worthy of note. If he hopes to get along with people, a person cannot expect always to have his own way. If one expects others to fall in line with him, he must be ready to yield on occasion to their way, even though he may not like it. Human relationship is a two-way traffic. One has to give in, in order to earn the right to receive. One has to make concessions to others in order to gain their support and cooperation. With respect to such things as essential principles or common welfare or the ultimate goal, it is desirable to have the courage of conviction and an unyielding strength of character. But with regard to matters of minor importance, such as a choice between more or less convenient or expedient lines of action, it is good to feel the pulse of the people and accept the dominant tendency. He leads best who is led by the welfare of all concerned. He loves best who follows the love of all he is dealing with. The spirit of accommodation combines within itself the opposite qualities of strength and mercy, unflinching devotion and loving submission. Strength of character and devotion to principle prevent the spirit of accommodation from degenerating into rank opportunism. Loving concern for the welfare of all would make the spirit of accommodation an effective means of fruitful cooperation, and not a tactical device for self-glorification.

Patanjali, the great teacher of Rāja Yoga, has mentioned an important principle of social relationship. It is the principle of non-acceptance of unnecessary gifts (*aparigraha*).* It has various implications. First, it is designed to prevent the tendency of carrying coal to Newcastle. Those who have enough and more begin to receive still more and attract all manner of gifts. This establishes the process of the rich getting richer and the poor getting poorer. This principle was dramatized in the life of Mahatma Gandhi in South Africa. When Gandhi was about to leave for India at the end of his service in South Africa as an attorney, members of the Indian community, rich and poor, showered all sorts of gifts upon him. After a night-long debate, Gandhi prevailed upon his wife in deciding not to accept those gifts

* Patanjali, *Yoga Sutras*, Sutra II.

for their personal use, and the objects were made into the nucleus of a public welfare fund to be used for the best interests of the Indian community in South Africa.

Secondly, this principle is intended to disapprove covetousness. There are people who have inordinate greed, who desire to get something for nothing, who are always on the lookout for special favors. This tendency is inimical to growth of character. It strikes at the root of one's independent stand in society. There is a special joy in being satisfied with what one earns honestly by his own effort. There is a greater joy in giving than in receiving dubious gifts. It is wise to be content with normal gifts of love from near and dear ones and from those who give unconditionally.

Thirdly, the principle is a guarantee of personal freedom and devotion to higher values. In our society gifts often assume the form of more or less subtle bribery. Behind them are lurking motives of undue influence, squeezing a special favor from the recipient or using him for some dirty work. You receive today an unexpectedly handsome gift from a fellow being. On the surface it looks wonderful—all kindness and sweetness. But a few days later he confronts you with a very difficult decision. He requests you, let us say, to do something involving injustice or untruthfulness, fraud or unkindness to a common friend. You feel extremely embarrassed. You don't know how to disoblige this donor nor how to disregard your sense of values. That is why it is so important to watch out for gifts to which strings, visible or invisible, might be attached. Dubious gifts are like the lure of the devil. They rob a person of his freedom and strength to speak out for the truth and fight for justice. So it is a sound principle not to accept any big gift when there is a reasonable doubt about the ultimate motive or about the danger of having to compromise one's sense of values.

In appreciation of the soundness of this principle, the governments of many countries, including the United States, have a ruling that government employees should not accept gifts from the public.

Another principle to remember in dealing with people is what we may call tactical toughness. There is no doubt that the ruling principle of life is based on love and kindness. This is rewarding not only spiritually but also pragmatically or in terms of social success. But precisely with a view to preserving the spirit of kindness in its full usefulness, a tough exterior has often to be put up. A tough exterior is a tactical device to keep at a distance aggressive and unscrupulous people. If a person is too soft on the surface, or overly kind in his outward behavior, he is likely to stimulate the exploitative instincts of certain people. Unconcealed sweetness is a temptation to the forces of evil. Love has to be protected with the voice of thunder.

An ancient Hindu story illustrates this point beautifully. One time a holy man was passing through a village. Some youngsters warned him not to go too near a particular old tree in the hollow trunk of which a giant serpent lived. Every now and then the serpent would come out of its dwelling place and work havoc by killing a goat or biting an unwary child. To the amazement of the children, the holy man headed right toward that very tree. He bent low and seemed to whisper something to the serpent. As he resumed his journey, the youngsters gathered around him and wanted to know what he had told the serpent. The holy man said that he had given the serpent the motto of love (*ahimsā*). He said to the serpent, "Look, you monster, you have been committing terrible sins by killing and poisoning sacred living things. If you want to be saved, you must start practicing, right from today, the motto of nonviolence." The holy man left the village, and the news of his visit spread. The next day the youngsters found the serpent meek as a lamb. Pretty soon they gathered courage and began to handle him roughly. One day they played tug-of-war with him, pulling at two ends. Once, they twisted him around a stick like a rope. Then one naughty boy swirled the snake and forcefully dashed him against the tree. After that they did not see the snake any more. Two weeks later when that holy man came back to the village, the boys reported to him the apparent death of the snake. When the holy man peeped into the hole of the tree, the coiled serpent, terribly emaciated, complained, "Look, sir, what your gospel of love has done to me. I am badly bruised and mutilated, and am about to die now." The holy man chided him by saying: "I told you not to bite any living creature. But why did you not hiss when you were attacked?"

Even when you don't mean to bite, you have on occasion to hiss. That is the language evildoers can easily understand. And that is the way the dignity of love can be vindicated. A soft heart needs a hard exterior.

CHAPTER VIII

The Meaning of Death

LIFE AND DEATH are two arms of the Lord of existence, Síva. With one arm he constantly creates life out of nothing. With the other arm he withdraws life into the abyss of nothingness, he dissolves all living forms into the formlessness of Being. New life springs out of the ashes of death. Death dogs the steps of life, spurs it to ever-new effort of conquest. Man is always ready to die in order to live the life of his dreams. And he lives in order to conquer death by the power of his being.

Every night man dies temporarily when he goes into the silence of sleep. Every morning he wakes up with new life. Every step he takes forward in his personality growth is an act of dying and being reborn. When he dies as a child, he is reborn as an adolescent. When he dies as an adolescent, he is reborn as a youth. When he dies as a youth, he is reborn as a mature adult. When he dies as an adult, he is reborn as a wise old man. This whole process of dying and being reborn in the course of continued growth is symbolized by the daily alternating phases of sleeping self-burial and wakeful self-assertion. If sleep is temporary death, death is the final sleep. The mystery of that final sleep has been the most baffling question before man throughout the ages. If daily living is the emergence from the self-burial of sleep, could it be that the final sleep is the preparation for a radically new mode of self-being?

Martin Heidegger has rightly pointed out that, for man, death is not merely the chronological end of his life. It is not just a stop to the process of life. It imparts to life its completion and fulfillment. Death turns life into a unified whole, a complete piece of music. The more a living person plans his living in communion with death, the more his life becomes a well-rounded aesthetic whole. The glory of life reaches its height in intelligent communion with death.

For man death is not merely an external end, waiting out there for the proper moment of life's completion. It does not simply stare life in the face from the outside. It penetrates into the very heart of life. It accompanies life as an invisible companion. Consciously or unconsciously, it determines the very style and pattern of living. The kind of life we live largely depends upon the kind of view we have of the meaning of death.

Man cannot afford to live like the animals in complete oblivion of the phenomenon of death. Fortunately or unfortunately, consciousness is the essential structure of his being. So at an early age the tremendous fact of death is thrust upon his attention, whether he likes it or not. But the majority of people try to suppress the issue which is so terribly disturbing. They fight shy of looking death squarely in the face. The inevitability of death is tucked away under the generalized formula "all men die." When death suddenly strikes in the neighborhood, there is a temporary shock followed by brief bereavement. But the matter is quickly disposed of with the help of some such abstract and impersonal piece of wisdom as "people die." Direct and personal confrontation with death is a tremendously overwhelming experience.

Most people cannot take it. Abstract and impersonal formulas come in handy as part of the defensive mechanism of the human psyche.

In the Hindu epic the Mahābhārata there is the interesting story about the riddle of death. Yudhisthira, who was wisdom and righteousness incarnate, went to drink water from a pond. He was extremely thirsty. But as he was about to drink he was challenged by a mysterious bird. He could not drink water from that pond unless he could give satisfactory answers to a few questions. All his brothers who previously drank from the same pond had dropped dead there on account of their failure to give right answers to the bird's questions. Now one of the questions Yudhisthira was asked was: "What is the most astonishing fact about human life?" Yudhiṣthira answered by saying, "Numberless living beings are passing out of existence every day, but still those who live act as if they would never die." What can be more astonishing than this ostrich-like policy toward the pervasive presence of death? The more a person suppresses the issue of death, the more unprepared he is to meet death gracefully. When one day death does actually knock at the door, one does not quite know what to do. There is fear and trembling in the presence of the unknown. There is overwhelming grief over lost opportunity or spoiled future. There is utter inability to accept death as a fitting curtain over the drama of life.

Death operates in the mind as a dark question mark. Is it the total annihilation of life with all its promise and potential, with all its hopes and aspirations? Or is it the gateway to a new phase of life fraught with new possibilities? A man's response to the question that death poses determines his entire mode of living.

DIFFERENT ATTITUDES TOWARD DEATH

Those who suppress the issue of death show a negative attitude. They act as if they were going to live forever. They pour out all the energy of life in building permanent castles on the quicksands of time. Possessiveness and acquisitiveness, greed and exploitation, craving for power and plenty, are their dominating impulses. The policy of suppression may be carried to such an extreme that one sincerely comes to believe that death is an illusion. Whatever may happen to others, they themselves are chosen individuals who think they will never die. It is only the ignorant who think they will die. Those who completely banish the thought of death from their minds conquer death thereby. Death being an illusion, it is only the idea of death which is real. Purged of all thoughts about the idea of death, a person is believed to become immortal.

There are some people who live in constant dread of death. But dread of death makes cowards of us all. And cowards die many times before their death. Fear of death paralyzes initiative and stifles the spirit of adventure. It prevents people from taking risks in life and thus strikes at the roots of progress. No risk, no gain. Only those can live to the height of their potentiality who are ready to die for the glory of life. Those who are constantly afraid of death, betray the poverty of life. They experience life at its lowest ebb and struggle to cling to it by all means. By failing to allow life to dare forth in the face of danger, they embrace living death. Failing to comprehend the imperishable value of life, they withdraw from all external hazards into an inert shell. Their love of life degenerates into blind attachment to an empty shell. Nothing can be more insulting to life than cowardly attachment.

If some people fail to live boldly, out of their fear of death, there are others who can lightly throw away life on account of a secret attraction toward death. Death is not all dreadful, popular belief notwithstanding. Death has also a sweet, fascinating aspect. It exercises a magnetic attraction upon the minds of many people, even though they may not be consciously aware of it. In poetic and mystical literature death has been eulogized as the great beloved. A Vaiṣṇava poet has sung:*

O death, thou art like unto my beloved Deity, Shyāma. (*Marana re, tuhu mama Shyama samān.*)

In addressing death as the beloved deity, the poet voices the unspoken sentiment of many people. Some people secretly long for death as a sweet escape from the horror of life. Life is reduced in their eyes to a nightmare. The pressures and problems of life prove too much for them. By comparison, death appears charming. Suicide frequently haunts the mind as the sweet solution to the conflicts and crises of life. For some again, life becomes emptied of all meaning. Divested of all charm and color, and reduced to nothingness, life stands stark naked before their disenchanted souls. The shocking experience of this naked nothingness—the unmitigated meaninglessness of life—drives the disenchanted to the path of slow, unconscious suicide. The religious practice of rigid austerity and self-mortification is the pseudo-mystical version of this suicidal policy. The peace of death is equated with the peace of pure

* Rabindranath Tagore (ed.), *Bhānusingher Padāvali* (Calcutta: Viswa Bharati, 1962), p. 33.

transcendence. The mystery of death is equated with the mystery of the great beyond.

For a great many people, the emotional reaction to death is ambivalent. Interwoven in it are feelings of love and hatred, of attraction and repulsion, of appreciation and rejection. To the conscious mind death is terrifying and repugnant. But to the unconscious mind death may be secretly fascinating and benevolent. When this ambivalent attitude is carried to an abnormal length, people live reckless and foolhardly lives. In a spirit of bravado, they rush in where angels fear to tread. They get kicks out of extremely dangerous situations. They are prone to have terrible accidents time and again.

There are cases of people who consciously make elaborate preparations to avoid untimely death. But those very preparations turn out to be an act of clearing the ground for death. An ancient story from the Masnavi tells of a nobleman who came to the court of Solomon in a state of great fear and agitation. Addressing the great King Solomon, he said, "My Lord, may I request you to save my life? Azrael, the angel of death, has looked upon me so angry and baleful!" "What do you want me to do to save your life?" asked the King. "Please command the wind to carry me to the heart of Hindustan this very day," was the nobleman's request. At the King's command the wind carried him softly and swiftly to the capital of India. A couple of hours later when the angel of death came to the court to pay his respects to the King, Solomon charged him: "Why did you frighten my faithful nobleman with your baleful look?" "Baleful look—not at all, my lord. I looked at him with great astonishment when I found him on the street of Baghdad. From Baghdad to India is a far cry.

God has commanded me to seize his spirit this very day in the heart of Hindustan."*

So the nobleman flies in a hurry from Baghdad to India precisely in order to meet his fate and keep his secret appointment with death. Death does indeed attract with a gravitational pull. Is it destiny? Or is it the secret longing of one's own unconscious? Perhaps it is both. Perhaps what is called destiny is the decree of one's own unconscious mind. Our destiny is indeed woven out of the invisible threads that emanate from our unconscious being.

Death, like Janus, has two faces. Death in its terrifying aspect appears to some as the cruel, punishing, overpowering father image. Death in its sweet and charming aspect represents the kind, captivating, ever-forgiving mother image. Ernest Jones has observed that it is this double, symbolical significance of death which provides the key to the understanding of Freud's ambivalent emotional attitude toward his own death.** On the one hand Freud had great fear of death. He was terribly afraid of growing old, according to his own testimony. For periods of time not a single day passed without his being obsessed with fearful ideas about death. He was in the most annoying habit of saying goodbye to his friends with the words, "You may not see me again." On the other hand he had a secret longing for death. He wanted to live only as long as his mother was alive. After his mother's death he would be happy to die peacefully. One time in 1912, when he regained consciousness after a fainting attack, his first remark was, "O death would be so sweet." After his mother's death, he thought, his

* A. J. Arberry, *Tales from the Masnavi* (London: George Allen & Unwin Ltd., 1961), p. 48.
** Ernest Jones, *The Life and Work of Sigmund Freud*, Vol. III (New York: Basic Books, 1957), p. 279.

death would amount to a peaceful reunion with her.

When there is deep and abiding love between two individuals, death emerges as the final and unbreakable seal of union between them. So lovers love to die together and rest together in the grave. Herein lies the explanation of the fact that when a lovable public figure dies or commits suicide, the event often gives rise to a strange suicidal wave. Those who identified themselves with him through love long to be united with him through death. This happened on a great scale with the early Christians who yearned to be united with Jesus through death. It happened also with many Buddhist monks in Asia. In South Vietnam an incredible suicidal wave was set off by the self-burning of a venerable Buddhist monk (Bonzai) for the sake of religious equality. Similar phenomena have been seen in the past after the death of some movie darling such as Rudolph Valentino.

It has already been noted that the vast majority of people fight shy of squarely facing the issue of personal death. But when once in a while an individual comes to grips with death personally, when he reflects upon the fact that one day, and that may be any day, he as a particular living individual will die and be done with, a profound change is likely to come over his whole attitude toward life. A new sense of urgency and seriousness is sure to be generated, a veil lifted from his vision of the meaning of life, and he has a new sense of liberation from the fetters of time.

EXISTENTIAL CONTACT WITH DEATH

Serious contemplation of death has been the beginning of man's most daring search for the truth. Existential contact with death has been the cause of the most profound transformation of human personality. So long as we behold death at a distance from a comfortable situation in life, it appears at best as a vague and mysterious future event. But when we encounter Death face to face and shake hands with him, some unsuspected springs of courage and creative imagination are likely to be tapped in us. As we take our stand in the heart of death, the deepest significance of life is likely to be revealed to us. The true meaning of life can indeed be comprehended only from the perspective of death. The essence of being can indeed be grasped only from the standpoint of nonbeing.

BUDDHA'S ENCOUNTER WITH DEATH

One day when the young prince Sidhārtha was walking the streets, he came upon the spectacle of death. A dead man was being carried in a coffin to the cremation ground. The spectacle moved the prince to the depths of his being. It immediately cast a thick, dark veil upon the entire face of life. It reduced to utter insignificance man's prodigious preparations for pomp and pleasure, for power and splendor. He resolved to renounce his kingdom in favor of an all-out search for life's ultimate meaning. In his quest of truth, he went to extreme lengths—to the extremes of rigorous austerity and self-destruction. But as he sat facing up to death at the end of prolonged fasting and penance, a new vision of the meaning of life dawned upon him. There was no truth on the path of self-mortification, he realized. Death discloses not only the vanity of life but also its supreme value. So the middle path has to be trodden—the path that steers clear of vainglorious self-deception on the one hand, and fruitless self-destruction on the other. The first encounter with death shocked Sidhārtha out of his emotional entanglements. It shattered the illusion of life being permanent. The second encounter with death opened his eyes to the intrinsic value of all life as the diversified expression of the nontemporal.

Sidhārtha met with death for the third time when he was seated under the Bodhi tree with a firm resolve to do or die. He was plunged in deep meditation. With unflinching devotion he was determined to attain the goal—the ideal of unclouded vision of the truth. As he made a determined effort to envision the ultimate, there appeared before him a terrific demon, the double-faced demon of Desire-Death (*Kāma-Māra*). The demon applied the age-old strategy of the carrot and the stick. On the one hand he promised Sidhārtha the richest treasures of the world and the most charming heavenly damsels, if only he would give up the mad pursuit of the key to the redemption of mankind. On the other hand, he threatened him with utter destruction if he chose the most unearthly path of supreme liberation from the bonds of the natural and the supernatural alike. The most terrible-looking hordes of the demon-king were ready to crush Sidhārtha. But Sidhārtha demonstrated his complete mastery over both desire and death. He disregarded the allurements as well as the intimidations of the deceitful demon. By showing complete fearlessness in his spiritual search for the supreme good, he conquered the power of death. When the spirit of man triumphs over death, nothing is impossible for him any more. Sidhārtha attained supreme enlightenment. By subduing death he gained profound insight into life's ultimate meaning.

It would be interesting to note that the Buddha, the

enlightened One, encountered death once more—for the fourth time—before his final departure. This time death appeared in the subtlest form, of desire—the most hidden and powerful desire of the individual soul. It is the desire for personal liberation, for the most transcendent joy and peace that an individual can attain. It is the desire for blissful self-absorption in the absolute. It is the desire for that eternal rest and peace from which death derives its secret fascination. Standing at the doorstep of formless liberation (*parinirvāna*), the Buddha paused and pulled back. Instead of entering into the transcendent peace of formless liberation, he took that famous vow which is known as the *Bodhisattva* vow. He decided to dedicate the rest of his life to the loving service of humanity, nay, of the entire living creation. It was the spectacle of suffering in life which drove him to the path of all-out spiritual search. It now became his paramount duty to play his part in eliminating the suffering of life, to sacrifice personal salvation at the altar of cosmic welware. There was to be no rest and peace for him so long as suffering should continue to afflict fellow beings. He was not to stop working until every suffering member of the living creation be brought to the path of *Nirvāna*—the path of light and love and joy.

Contemplation of death may produce complete disenchantment with life. It shakes loose all bonds of attachment to the earth and drives individuals to look for something permanent beyond life and death. That is how the intensely religious mood is often born. In recent times an example of this has been furnished by Ramana Maharshi, the sage of Arunachal.

RAMANA MAHARSHI'S ENCOUNTER WITH DEATH

In 1896, when Ramana was only seventeen years old, he was sitting one day all alone on the first floor of his uncle's house, in perfectly good health. Suddenly he felt that he was going to die. So his whole mind was engaged upon the meaning of death. What happens to a man when he dies? His body is carried stiff to the cremation ground and consigned to the flames. But does his inmost core, the I, also perish in the process? That depends upon what precisely is meant by the I. So immediately he proceeded with all the concentrated force of his intelligence to investigate into the ultimate meaning of the I. He dramatized the scene of death. He stretched out in imitation of a corpse, held his breath, closed his mouth, pressed his lips tightly together.*

Then his vital energies were withdrawn from the body and gathered into the mind and turned inward, animated by the burning desire to find the real Self, if any. "At this moment a mysterious power rose up from the innermost core of his being and took complete possession of the whole mind and life; by that power he, —that is to say, his mind and life—was taken inwards."** Possessed by this power, his mind plunged deep into the ultimate source of life and mind and was merged in It. This was the egoless and mindless state of illumination. This was the sage's existential experience of the nontemporal. On the attainment of enlightenment, all doubt disappeared and all fear including the fear of death completely vanished. The deathless center of existence was contacted. The true self was realized as

* B. V. Narasimha Swami, *Self-Realisation*, 6th ed. (Tiruvannamalai: Sri Ramanasramam, 1962), pp. 20-23.
** "WHO," *Maha Yoga* (Tiruvannamalai: Sri Ramanasramam, 1947), p. 6.

the self-shining Sun. All thoughts that would hencefor-
ward arise in the mind, and all actions that would hence-
forward be performed by the body, were experienced as
clouds covering the sky without in the least affecting the
Sun. In the words of Ramana Maharshi, it is a Natural
State of the Self (Sahaja Bhāva).*

How do you explain the sudden fear of death that
overwhelmingly seized the mind of the young Ramana
in his healthful adolescence? The whole affair, including the dramatization of death, the inquiry into I, the
withdrawal of all life force into the mind, the emergence of a mysterious indwelling power, the entire dissolution of mind and life, the final attainment of
illumination, was a very effortless and spontaneous unfoldment. No conscious planning or deliberate effort
was involved in the matter. Perhaps the sudden fear of
death that triggered the whole process was the mysterious pull of the nontemporal felt on the mental level.
From the very beginning his life was flowing in that
direction. The more a growing individual becomes ripe
for the inward pull of the eternal—for the grace of God
—the more the outward experiences of death and suffering become occasions for philosophic contemplation or
mystical adventure. The more an individual gets close
to the eternal, the more he dies in a very important
sense to the world of common experience. The lightning flash of spiritual insight strikes dead the natural
man with his natural mind and ego. The natural man
invariably dies in order to live the deathless life of the
spirit.

* *Ibid.*, p. 8.

DEATH AND REVOLUTION

Now instead of producing disenchantment with life, contemplation of death may also intensify the self-assertion of life. Instead of producing sages, it may create revolutionaries. The writings of modern existentialist thinkers bear this out. The last two great World Wars with mass destruction and massacre of the innocent have driven home the reality of death as life's next-door neighbor. Amidst the scenes of wanton slaughter and ruthless torture, the inevitability of death has been wrought into the innermost core of sensitive minds. Some people react against this situation by resolving to live desperately and dangerously. Out of naked exposure to death is born the death-defying spirit of revolution. There is fear of death so long as death is a remote possibility. After a man sees the naked face of death, there is no more fear. He can now fearlessly push forward to fathom the mystery of death and become a sage. But he may also fearlessly proceed to champion the cause of life, challenging death to a showdown. He is ready to die to promote the best interests of natural life, of life in the world. It is the death-defying spirit which has been at the source of the freedom movement of every modern nation. In every modern country thousands of people, young and old, have sacrificed their lives with a smiling face at the altar of their country's freedom.

DEATH AND INWARD TRANSFORMATION

I am reminded of a story which illustrates how confrontation with death changes one's whole perspective on life. A middle–aged man, very peevish, used to be upset by whatever would go contrary to his will. In the morning he prepared his tea with just the right amounts of cream and sugar. But once he found it was not sugar but salt. So he lost his temper and raised a storm. Who put salt in the sugar bowl? He scolded his wife and children. At night when he went to brush his teeth, he found that his toothpaste had been squeezed by somebody at the wrong place—in the middle instead of at the bottom. Who can tolerate such foolishness? Came a day he fell seriously ill. He was taken to the hospital and cancer was suspected. Doctors seemed to consider it a serious case without much hope for his life. So he found himself at death's door, listening to its dark whispers. He brought himself around eventually to accept the fact. With a fresh feeling of psychological readjustment, he lay serenely on his deathbed, looking out his window into the gathering darkness of the evening. He beheld how, one after another, the lights of the whole town were kindled, each dispelling a little darkness around it. Outside he could hear the maddening noise of revelers. Inside the hospital he could hear the cries of the sick and the agony of the dying. After midnight all sounds seemed to be hushed into dead silence. In the early hours of the morning, all the lights of the town went out again, one after another. The entire landscape he was watching appeared to epitomize the ultimate meaning of life in the universe. The lives of countless individuals are lighted in the world one after another. They begin to shine in the background of immeasurable darkness. There is an exuberance of excitement and adventure. There are tears and laughter in day-to-day affairs. But after a brief interval all the lives are finished, and melt into the all-encompassing darkness. That is how he felt.

Next day there was a thorough medical examination.

The findings disclosed that the suspected cancer was a psychosomatic symptom. The man was destined to live after all. So he was released from the hospital. But he went back home a radically changed person. Nothing can cause an angry ripple on the calm surface of his mind any more. Sugar or salt, kindness or cruelty, favor or frown, he keeps his peace of mind under all circumstances. He reacts to all situations, agreeable or disagreeable, with the serenity of his timeless perspective. Nothing can make him fly into a temper any more. Confrontation with death has given him the power of meeting life's opposites with serene understanding.

PRACTICE OF MEDITATION ON DEATH

There is a system of spiritual practice in India—especially in the Tāntric tradition—in which direct confrontation with death is prescribed as a part of meditation. The corpse or the skull as a symbol of death is used as an essential ingredient of the practice. One usually goes alone to the cremation ground on a dark night and takes his seat quietly for meditation in the midst of the frightening sights and sounds of death. The idea is to look at life from the standpoint of death—to contemplate the cycle of life and death in the context of the eternal. Several ideas start coming to the mind while sitting thus right in the house of death. One is that all men are equal here. All men, rich and poor, high and low, king and beggar, victor and vanquished—all are eventually turned to dust and reabsorbed into the womb of the same mother earth. All artificial distinctions of status and rank are nullified here. A few days earlier or later, death comes equally to all, irresistibly and remorselessly. The illusion of physical immortality is shattered.

Another idea that sharply pierces the mind is that of the vanity of much human living, and of the nothingness of much human emotion. Greed and acquisitiveness, lust and possessiveness, hatred and violence, jealousy and vengeance, exploitation and aggressiveness, are elemental drives of life. They thrive under the illusion of immortality. They vanish like mist before the rising sun through a shocking encounter with death. The timeless perspective that belongs to the dwelling place of death dissolves the cobwebs of emotional involvement. Individual lives are felt as bubbles on the ocean of time.

CONQUEST OF DEATH

Cut asunder from the emotional bonds of time, a person begins to feel the transcendent pull of the eternal. The more his horizon is expanded to embrace the vast immensity of time, the more he begins to glimpse the timeless essence of his own being. As a person grasps the reality of death as an essential component of life, he wakes up on the nontemporal dimension of his existence. The nontemporal is perceived as the substratum of both life and death. If life is negated in death, death is negated in the nontemporal. When death is negated, life is reaffirmed as it is, not as immortal existence but as an ever-changing field of manifestation of the never-ending glories of the eternal.

There is the fear of death so long as the self is unconsciously identified with the body. When the body is clearly seen as a body, that is to say as a changing, growing, declining, perishable thing functioning as an instrument of self-expression, the fear of death turns into an earnest desire to make use of the body at its maximum potential within the framework of its own limitations. With the illusion of personal immortality gone, the frenzied efforts at self-perpetuation and self-aggrandizement dry up at the source.

When the self is known as the self, that is to say not as the body nor as an object or thing but as a center of awareness of such higher values as truth, beauty, love, justice and freedom, death loses its terror. Death has its power only over the body which is born and which surely one day dies. But death has no power over the self which is identified with eternal values. The fundamental spiritual task of life is to put forth one's best efforts to fulfill in some degree the values which he beholds in his inner soul. If in that effort he fails, failure will be a stepping stone to future success. If in that effort he dies, death will be a gateway to immortality. To the extent to which he succeeds in that effort, his life becomes glorious.

CHAPTER IX

Meditating for Self-Perfection

MEDITATION IS THE ART of deeper self-awareness. It aims at the awareness of the self on subtle levels of personality. It culminates in the realization of the inmost center of one's own being. In realizing his inmost center of being, the individual attains self-fulfillment by transcending the fetters of the ego. He is released from the prison of egocentricity. He discovers that transcendental dimension of his existence which unites him with all other individuals.

In the external world there are different individualized material objects such as a grain of sand, a piece of coal, a slab of rock, a block of marble. If any one of them could get to know its inmost essence, it would realize itself as a specific configuration of space-time. Such realization would also disclose that all material objects are unified in space-time inasmuch as they are different configurations of the same space-time. Similarly when a human individual gets to know his inmost spiritual essence, he realizes himself as the focalized expression of the one, all-embracing, cosmic consciousness. This realization discloses his essential identity with all other human individuals, because all humans are in their inward essence different focalizations of the same cosmic consciousness.

Meditation is a kind of inner dialogue. It is a dialogue between the mind and its unconscious depths. It opens up lines of communication with the voice of Being as the deepest center of individual existence. Through such inner communication, the meaning of life, the purpose of existence, becomes more and more clear. A definite sense of direction is gained. An increasing harmony is established between the conscious and the unconscious aspects of personality. Finally, the harmonization of personality produces a penetrative insight into the super-personal ground of existence. The super-personal is that nontemporal dimension of our being which is the meeting ground of time and eternity. It is the source of all higher values. Active contact with the super-personal clothes life with a new meaning and significance. A transvaluation of the values of life takes place. A luminous transfiguration of personality is achieved. Springs of unmotivated love and creative joy are opened. Such love and joy do not depend upon any objective condition or external circumstance. They do not depend upon the fulfillment of any wish or expectation. They do not need any justification or external stimulus. They spontaneously well up from the depths of one's being, because they belong to the essence of being itself.

The image of the Buddha in meditation is a perfect expression of self-integration with the nontemporal dimension of existence. His eyes are half-opened and half-closed. While his left hand is turned inward, touching his body, his right hand is held aloft in the gesture of bestowing blessings upon the world. Half-closed eyes symbolize his blissful communion with the depths of his being, his integration with the eternal, his union with the super–personal. The joy and serenity of such inward

integration is reflected in his face and also in the indrawn gesture of his left hand. Half-opened eyes symbolize his loving communication with the universe, his
selfless compassion for all living creation. He is ready to
give himself in the service of humanity, nay, in the service of all living creatures. But to such self-giving there
is no string attached, no expectation of reward or recognition, no ulterior motivation. Discovery of the super-
personal ground of existence fills the mind with boundless love. The right hand with its bliss-bestowing gesture
beautifully reflects that selfless spirit of love and compassion (*karunā*).

The Buddha in the posture of meditation is the perfect picture of the extroverted introvert. Meditation is
the ingoing movement of consciousness. It explores the
inner regions of the mind with a view to self-integration
and the eventual discovery of the nontemporal ground
of existence. On the realization of the nontemporal
dimension, the essential identity of the individual and
the universal (Ātman and Brahman) is vividly perceived. The spiritual oneness of all existence is lumi-
nously apprehended. In consequence, meditation culminates in universal compassion. On gaining the inmost
center of existence, one's consciousness begins to expand
with the expansive urge of love. The seemingly contra-
dictory tendencies of introversion and extroversion are
perfectly harmonized in a balanced self-poise. In the
unity of wisdom and compassion (*prajñā* and *karunā*),
they are held in perfect equilibrium. They operate spontaneously like the inhaling and the exhaling, the systole
and the diastole, of integrated living. Intelligent communion with one's depth of being and loving communication with the outside world supplement each other in
illuminated living.

But how do you practice meditation as the art of communion with the ultimate ground of existence? How does it differ from prayer? How does it differ from thinking and reflection? How does it differ from concentration or visualization? How does it differ from phenomenological self-inquiry?

MEDITATION AND PRAYER

As a first step in grasping the essence of meditation, we may start with the observation that in prayer we talk to God, whereas in meditation we allow God to talk to us. The aim of meditation is to put a stop to the constant chattering of the mind and to establish silence there. In the depth of silence of one's being the soundless voice of Being is likely to be heard.

There are different types of prayer. First, there is the prayer of petition for material values. One prays to God for daily bread, for wealth and prosperity, for health and longevity, for success and security. In doing so one looks upon God as the heavenly Father or the heavenly Mother and exercises one's right as a child of the Divine. Prayer is an appeal to the paternal love, mercy, and justice of the Godhead.

Secondly, there is the prayer of thanksgiving and adoration. In prayer one offers thanks to God for the manifold blessings of life. One sings the praise of God and composes hymns of adoration. It is recognized that life in this world faces all kinds of dangers and threatening forces of destruction. It is the boundless love of Providence that gives protection to all living creatures and sustains them in their existence and growth. Reflection upon this fact fills the mind with a deep sense of gratitude. Prayer expresses that feeling of gratitude.

Thirdly, there is the prayer of longing for higher spiritual values. One begins to pray to God now not for wealth and prosperity but for wisdom and enlightenment. One prays not for success and security but for purity and love, for the delight of closeness to God. One realizes at this stage that man does not live by bread alone. At the higher stage of inner evolution, the hunger of the soul comes to the foreground and demands satisfaction. Preoccupation with material values is felt as an obstruction to the aspiration of the soul. One is now ready to set aside personal wishes and desires, with a view to grasping the will of God. Egoistic impulses impede the mind's vision of the divine truth.

But prayer reaches its purest form when one is able to say sincerely, "Let Thy will, not mine, be done." The noblest kind of prayer consists in getting into the mood of absolute receptivity and self-opening to the divine will. As soon as the divine will is disclosed in our consciousness, it should be accepted as the most dynamic force in our life. It should be accepted as the chief motivating factor in all actions. If one has any doubt as to how to go about it, one may pray to God to be able to pray right. In the view of Kierkegaard, that is the only real form of prayer.* It is through an act of self-offering to the Divine that the divine power can be brought into overt operation in our nature. And it is with the help of the divine power alone that the right relationship can be established between man and God. Prayer in its highest form is that right relationship.

When prayer assumes the form of silent self-opening and total self-surrender to the Divine, true meditation begins. When a person sincerely says, "Let Thy will, not

---

* Perry D. LeFevre, *The Prayers of Kierkegaard* (Chicago: The University of Chicago Press, 1956), p. 202.

mine, be done," he stops talking. He rises above the tumult of desire and the clamor of the ego and gets ready to listen to the voice of truth and love in the stillness of the heart. In doing so he undergoes a revolutionary change of consciousness, a Copernican revolution in his outlook on life. He passes from the egocentric to the cosmocentric outlook. He discovers the center of gravity of his being in the divine purpose of his life.

Meditation is an all-out search for the ultimate truth. It is a search for the truth about oneself and one's relationship to the universe. It is a search for the ground of existence and the meaning of life. In this radical spiritual quest, not only all egotistic impulses and desires, but also all preconceived notions and ideas have to be sacrificed to the mystic fire of the all-consuming passion for truth. Fixed ideas and unconscious intellectual assumptions are the last impediments to the unclouded vision of truth.

Prayer even in its highest form centers around the concept of God as an article of faith. God is accepted on the authority of the scriptures or the prophets or the Messiah. One may not as yet have any direct personal experience or realization of the divine reality. One may, on the contrary, have a sense of dualism or separation between the human individual who prays and the divine personality to whom prayer is directed. Thus prayer moves on the mental, dualistic level. It is sustained and nourished by certain theological beliefs about man, God, and their interrelationship. Faith in the personality of God and His sovereignty over man gives support to the act of prayer.

Meditation as a radical spiritual venture shakes loose from all fixed beliefs and theological assumptions. In meditation it is not necessary that one must have faith in God, let alone any specific theological doctrine about God. The purpose of meditation is to find out the ultimate truth and the ground of all being, setting on one side all preconceived notions and traditional beliefs about God. One may be a skeptic, an atheist, or an agnostic. But still he can engage in meditation provided he has a genuine desire to discover the truth about himself and about the foundation of his existence. He starts with such nontheological questions as "Who am I?" "What is the inmost center of my being?" "How am I related to the universe?"

The aim of meditation is to transform mere faith into living experience, into the direct and immediate experience of the ground of being. Belief in God accepted on authority turns into intimate realization of the ultimate meaning of God. The sense of dualism that separates the human soul from the universal reality is dissolved. Concepts, dogmas, doctrines and creeds which used to masquerade as the supreme truth are transcended. All anthropomorphic images of the eternal are consigned to the flames. The process of meditation culminates in the nondualistic experience of pure existence. The individual psyche and the cosmos are revealed as inseparably interrelated aspects of one, indivisible Being. New ideas and values appropriate to a particular historical epoch emerge from such direct meditational contact with Being.

MEDITATION AND REFLECTION

How does meditation differ from reflection and thinking? Reflection is an activity of the conscious, rational mind. It results in intellectual knowledge about that upon which reflection is directed. For instance, reflection upon the notion of God may result in perfectly systematized knowledge about God as an all-powerful, all-wise, and all-good Creator of the universe. Or, it may even result in the highly sophisticated conception of God as the Absolute Spirit of which the world is a mode of phenomenal manifestation. But for all such systematized knowledge about God, a person may not have any direct realization of God. He may suffer from unresolved emotional conflicts within himself. His intellectual brilliance may be accompanied by emotional immaturity. He may have that bitterness in his soul which sets him in opposition to the rest of the world. In his intellectual conceit, he may look down upon the world from his ivory tower of contemplation, supremely unconcerned about the weal and woe of the world. With all his mastery over words and concepts, he may be the slave of uncontrollable impulses. Like a vulture, however high he may soar upon the wings of speculation, his gaze may remain fixed upon the rotten carcass below.

Meditation aims at eliminating all discrepancies between intellect and emotion, between reason and passion. It opens up channels of communication between the conscious mind and the unconscious psyche. The aim is to allow the rational mind to come to terms with the forces of the unconscious, and to allow the unconscious to organize these impulses and urges in harmony with the central purpose of life. The increasing unification of the conscious and unconscious aspects of personality leads to an awakening of the cognitive power of the total self. It lifts the veil of ignorance and reveals the secret of man's rootedness in the universal.

While reflection is a function of the intellect, meditation is an integrative movement of consciousness, a function of the total self. Meditation begins as an effort to integrate the personality. It ends up as the unified truth-vision of the integrated personality. In the kind of enlightenment that meditation produces, intellect, emotion, impulse and action are brought together in dynamic harmony, giving an existential basis to thinking so that life and thought may not pull in opposite directions. In the course of the practice of meditation, a person learns to live more and more in the categories of his thought and to think more and more with his entire being.

It may thus be noted that meditation is existential reflection. Through meditation an individual tries to live his philosophy. He tries to put into practice in daily living what he thinks to be true. On the other hand, his thinking is directed to a clarification of the fundamental issues of life, to an increasing understanding of the problems, the values, and the presuppositions of actual living.

Meditation is radical reflection. Ordinary reflection is secretly determined by cultural provincialism and unconscious motivation. It is unconsciously determined by physiological processes. It has been rightly observed that a man's world-view is largely determined by the condition of his liver and the amount of his bank balance. A person with a damaged liver is likely to have a pessimistic world-view. A person with a negative bank balance may become either a desperate revolutionary or an enthusiast of the supernatural kingdom. A person's ideas of after-life, heaven, hell, God, devil, reward and punishment, are largely a result of his unconscious, wishful thinking. His inner frustrations unconsciously color his notions about them.

His personal unconscious is in turn largely determined by the collective unconscious of the community to which he belongs. His thinking about God, people, and events is more or less somnambulistically carried on within the framework of the ground conceptions provided by his social environment, or the religious community to which he belongs. Meditation is an endeavor to pierce these barriers of conditioning. Through self-transcendence, it unveils the unconscious motivations of ordinary thought and conduct. It helps transcend the tacit presuppositions of the traditional outlook. By means of deeper self-awareness, it removes the distorting factors in the psycho-physical apparatus. By means of radical criticism, it makes an unbiased examination of the ground conceptions of different cultural systems of the world. Finally it reveals the pragmatic character of such ground conceptions. It explores the myth of their absoluteness or sacrosanct infallibility. The ruling ethico-religious ideas of different communities have only relative validity and limited application under certain social, economical, and political conditions. Thus meditation produces a spiritual outlook which is in a sense beyond good and evil. It enables an individual to think as a citizen of the world, not as an emotionally fixated member of a given community. It enables a person to speak with the voice of universal truth and to champion the cause of cosmic welfare.

Finally, meditation is self-transcending reflection. All reflection involves a dichotomy—the dichotomy of subject and object. When a person thinks, he thinks about something concerning himself or the world around him. His thinking discloses the whole world including himself as the object of his thoughts. His own ideas, feelings, wishes, joys, sorrows, love and hatred, knowledge and ignorance, activity and idleness, can all, in ultimate analysis, be said to belong in the realm of the objective.

But as the thinker, the pure subject, he somehow stands above and outside of the whole world, including his own psychological being or mind-body continuum. The pure subject is a transcendental act of awareness, which in its essence is emptiness or no-thing-ness. If it be viewed as some-thing, some actual psychic event or act or process, it can be reflected upon and turned into an object of thought. In that case it ceases to be pure subject. The pure subject is therefore no-thing, no-object. It is the presupposition of all thinking about things and objects. It is like the eye that can never see itself. As the light of all lights, it shines by its own intrinsic light.

Thus meditation reveals transcendental awareness as the most distinctive characteristic of man. Transcendental awareness contains the seed of perfection in him. It accounts for his infinite perfectibility. It opens for him the path toward infinite progress. By virtue of transcendental awareness, man becomes aware of his limitations. To cognize a limitation is, in a sense, to transcend it. Limitation limits so long as one is an unconscious victim thereof. The moment we become aware of a limitation, we go beyond it. Either we make an effort to eliminate it or uproot it, or we develop a compensatory virtue that outbalances it. Or we reconcile ourselves to it and thus release our energy for some other, more fruitful achievement. For instance, so long as a person is not aware of his evil temper, he operates unredeemably under its baleful influence. But awareness of his evil temper enables him to half-conquer it. He may seek help from a spiritual teacher or competent psychotherapist for the cure of his emotional imbalance. He may avoid circumstances which emotionally disturb him. The deepening light of self-awareness born of the regular practice of meditation may eventually spot and scorch the psychic roots of evil temper.

Meditation is indeed an excellent training in transcendental awareness. By virtue of such training, one can overcome the relativity of thought and existence, and penetrate to that ultimate ground from which both emerge as interrelated factors.

Idealism posits thought or idea as the creative center of all existence. The entire existing world is believed to be sustained by the power of thought. There is certainly an element of truth in this idealistic contention. But it is equally true, as existentialism points out, that thought in its turn presupposes existence. I think, because I am. Meditation provides an ontological breakthrough here. By the power of meditation one can rise above the polarized structure of thought and existence, of consciousness and reality, and contact the indeterminable Being which is the ground of both. The existing world is the manifestation of Being in space-time. Thought or consciousness is the reflection of the light of Being on highly evolved and transparent organisms like men. Thus out of meditation is born that profound wisdom which discloses the ultimate truth in which idealism and existentialism are reconciled.

STEPS OF MEDITATION

Now what are the essential factors involved in the practice of meditation? How does one go about it?

Since meditation aims at the truth-vision of one's integrated personality, it cannot be just the exercise of any isolated faculty of the mind. It is the spiritual reorganization of one's whole life. Broadly speaking, it involves the following seven factors: (1) the spirit of moderation or the middle path; (2) bodily discipline; (3) practice of concentration; (4) detached self-observation; (5) discernment and critical evaluation; (6) enlightenment; and (7) dedication to cosmic welfare.

(1) *The Spirit of Moderation.* Passion and reason, impulse and law, nature and spirit, have to be brought into a dynamic harmony. The life of passion without the guidance of reason leads to self-dissipation. It loses itself in the chaos of conflicting impulses. It squanders energy. In treading the path of selfishness, it cuts itself off from all sources of higher inspiration. On the other hand, the life of pure reason, without the drive and delight, the freshness and spontaneity provided by passion, leads to self-mutilation. By suppressing the instinctual urges, it destroys the springs of action and kills the joy of living. It brings on sterility and produces a drab, colorless personality. It strikes at the root of warmth and enthusiasm which make for creativity. It piles up inner tension and conflict which can easily lead to a breaking point. In treading the path of abstract rationalism and asceticism, it uproots the self from the soil of the vital impetus.

The task of meditation is to organize one's fundamental impulses and drives intelligently in accordance with the central ideal of life. When the demands of the unconscious psyche are accepted in principle, the privations involved in self-discipline become tolerable. When both passion and reason are recognized in the scheme of living, inner conflicts are kept at a minimum. Whatever psychic tensions may arise from the conduct of the daily affairs of life, can then be easily endured. There is a built-in device in the psyche for converting failures and frustrations into the creative energies of renewed effort.

There is also a built-in mechanism for continuous transition from the satisfaction of one set of desires to the emergence of nobler and finer desires, from the fulfillment of one set of values to the unfoldment of a new set of higher values.

The mediating power of meditation is also manifested in the shape of non-action in action. It steers the middle course between the extroverted and introverted tendencies of human nature.

There are some people who become too involved in the activities of life. They impulsively do things for which they must repent later on when it is too late. While in action they seem to be helplessly driven by the force of impulse to undesirable lengths. Instead of acting, they feel themselves as slaves of action. The threads of action are more and more interwoven into a terrible noose around their necks. On the other hand, there are people who decide to withdraw from the field of action. They choose the path of negation, the path of inaction or quietism. In nostalgic fashion they yearn for the undifferentiated oneness of the infantile mind. They long to return to the blissful security of the mother's lap, either in the quiet solitude of the mountain cave or the peaceful silence of the burial ground. While the extrovert ignores the psychic depth of personality, the introvert ignores the social horizon of personal life.

Human personality is psycho-social in structure. Meditation is the art of harmonizing the social and the psychical aspects of personality. In order to do so, meditation aims at developing the spirit of serene self-poise in the midst of all action. Sri Krishna expresses the essence of meditation in a nutshell when he says to Arjuna in the Bhagavad-Gītā, "Be united with the Divine and act." To participate in social action in the spirit of union with the eternal is indeed of the essence of meditation. To be united with the eternal is to place truth and love above the self. All personal activities and egotistic promptings are consumed in the mystic fire of that union. Action grounded upon such union is the working out of truth and love. The personal equation is at a discount. The little self is set at naught. The self acts and yet it does not act. It acts insofar as it is identified with the values that emerge out of union with the eternal. It does not act insofar as all the selfish motives are sacrificed at the altar of higher values. Identification with values of eternity produces boundless freedom and blissful self-poise. The liquidation of selfish motives secures liberation from fear and anxiety, from attachment and impatience. Meditation prevents action from becoming compulsive and self-consuming. It prevents contemplation from becoming permanently aloof, withdrawn and inactive. It gradually bridges the gulf between outward action and inward peace. It illuminates action with the light of deeper self-awareness. It calms action with the power of contemplation. On the other hand, by transforming contemplation into direct contact with the eternal, it establishes truth and love as the most dynamic forces of life.

(2) *Bodily Discipline.* Since meditation is the unified functioning of the total personality, emphasis must be laid upon the need for adequate bodily discipline. The body has to be carefully built up as a fit and strong instrument of higher spiritual living. Body and mind are inseparably intertwined, interrelated aspects of the continuum of existence.

There are some who attach exaggerated importance to the body. They proceed to develop the muscles of the body at the cost of the brains. They spend hours in

beautifying the body while ignoring the beautiful qualities of the soul. They may even devote a whole life to
the practice of very elaborate and intricate bodily postures and exercises in the belief that that, alone, is sufficient for spiritual unfoldment.

On the other hand, there are people who consider the
body a positive impediment to spiritual growth. They
look upon the body as a burden upon the soul, or as a
prison house. At its best, the body is used as a ladder
upon which one can climb up to the roof of spiritual
glory. On reaching the contemplated heights of spiritual
achievement, it does not matter if the body falls to
pieces. Some seem to think that since they are interested
in the development of the spirit, they can afford to let
the body go to the dogs. So they practice all manner of
self-denying ordinances including prolonged fasting,
sleepless nights, indifference to the rules of hygiene.
Some again take care of the body to the extent to which
and as long as it may serve as a means of realizing God.
As soon as the spiritual goal it attained, the sooner the
spirit is released from the mortal coils, the better.

Those who pamper the body and those who punish
the body are equally in the wrong. The body is to be
built up in strength and health, not for its own sake, but
for the sake of higher values—the values of social service
and cultural pursuits. Even after the profoundest spiritual fulfillment, the body has a vastly important function to fulfill. It is not only a means of union with the
eternal, but also a medium of manifesting the glory of
the eternal in life and society. If a person neglects the
body in the course of his spiritual pursuits, he contracts
disease. When a genuine spiritual experience comes, his
body, already debilitated, may give way under its overwhelming impact. He fails to absorb quietly the new

spiritual experience with its powerful emotional impact, which may even prove shattering to the nervous system, resulting in derangement and psychic disorientation. It is neglect of the body which renders it a burden or a prison house. Truly speaking, the body is intended to be an effective means of communication with the outside world, a powerful instrument of creative action. Meditation is the art of developing the body potential to its highest. To that end the Gītā says one should eat neither too much nor too little. One should sleep neither too much nor too little.* One should not exert oneself too much nor abstain from all exertion or exercise. One must intelligently make use of the latest findings of hygiene, medicine, dietetics, and the like to develop the body into a strong and healthy instrument of one's central ideal of life.

(3) *Concentration.* Concentration is an essential step in meditation. It consists in mobilizing the resources of the mind in one direction. It is the training in the focusing of mental energy upon one definite target. It consists in withdrawing the mind from all irrelevant things and holding attention upon a chosen interest. Concentration turns the mind into a powerful searchlight. Ordinarily the mind is like a candle or a kerosene lamp. The rays of consciousness are diffused in all directions. Attention gallops on the surface of things without hitting any depth. But the concentrated mind acquires the power of penetrating to the inmost essence of a thing like a powerful searchlight.

Concentration assumes various forms such as intellectual, aesthetic, practical, religious, and yogic. By virtue of his training in intellectual concentration, the scientist fathoms the mysteries of the atom on the one

* The Bhagavadgītā, VI, 16.

hand, and the expanding universe with its moving galaxies on the other. By virtue of his training in aesthetic concentration, the artist becomes one with the spirit of nature. Through concentration upon a flower he becomes one with it. Through concentration upon a landscape he becomes one with the landscape. He then allows the spirit of the flower or the landscape which has penetrated his mind to express itself through him in his specific artistic medium, whether painting or poetry or sculpture.

The socially successful man, the politician or the captain of industry, practices concentration in the form of visualization. He forms a clear picture in his mind of exactly what he wants. Then he proceeds with unswerving determination to mobilize all his resources and adopt suitable means toward the actualization of his mental project. He does not allow any distraction or irrelevant consideration to stand in his way.

The religious man concentrates upon such religious symbols as the Buddha figure, the Christ figure, the cross, the wheel, the star of David, the crescent moon, the Krishna figure, the Yam-Yin symbol, and so on. Since his concentration is more emotional than intellectual, he becomes more and more one with the symbol, resulting in intense religious devotion and enthusiasm.

Religious concentration differs from scientific, aesthetic, and pragmatic forms of concentration in its emotional content. A scientist or an artist or a businessman may be very successful in his field and yet be a great atheist or skeptic. But a religious man is a man of faith. He believes his idol to be an emblem of absolute truth, goodness, and love, a deathless symbol of God.

Nonreligious concentration may be ethically neutral

or even evil. A person may plan to rob a bank or murder a competitor. He may successfully carry out his plan by virtue of his immense power of concentration or visualization, with meticulous attention paid to the minutest details of its execution. Concentration becomes religious only when it is guided by a sense of higher values. Meditation as a spiritual act is the channeling of concentration to the divine or to the eternal.

When religious concentration is predominantly emotional, with the critical intelligence set aside, it exalts or magnifies the symbol above the reality behind it. The distinction between the symbol and the symbolized is ignored. As a result, religious concentration may lead to dogmatism, sectarianism, fanaticism, and the like.

But religious concentration may also combine intellect and emotion in a balanced harmony. Feelings of love, reverence, and loyalty may be combined with intellectual analysis, comparison, evaluation, or criticism. In that case religious concentration assumes the form of yogic concentration. Yogic concentration may start with any of the religious symbols mentioned above. But its aim is finally to penetrate to the universal reality beyond the particular symbol. For instance, although it may start with the symbols of the Christ figure, the Buddha figure, or the Krishna figure, it ultimately aims to go beyond such symbols to that universal principle— the principle of cosmic love and wisdom—of which Buddha, Christ, and Krishna are historical manifestations.

Yogic concentration may, in fact, start with any kind of symbol, religious or nonreligious. It may begin with a flower as a symbol of pure love, or with flame as a symbol of light and knowledge, or with the ocean as a symbol of cosmic consciousness in which all creatures live, move, and have their being, or with the mountain as a symbol of the sublime which is at once daunting and fascinating. Through concentration, the practitioner seeks to become one with the ultimate source of such values as love, wisdom, beauty, sublimity. Yogic concentration may also begin by focusing attention upon the flow of one's breath, or upon a particular center of consciousness such as the heart center. I have discussed different methods of concentration in detail elsewhere.* By virtue of such concentration, the central psychophysical power, the Kuṇḍalinī, is awakened. The dormant spiritual energy is activated. By means of proper channeling, this awakened energy goes to activate the unused cells of the brain, galvanizing the entire nervous system and eventually opening the doors of man's deepest spiritual insight. Ordinary religious categories are incapable of describing the ultimate dimension of Being. It is neither God nor soul but that pure Transcendence which is the unitary basis of both God and soul, of both the universal and the individual.

(4) *Detached self-observation.* Another method of meditation lies in a direction that is radically different from concentration. It is the method of letting go, the method of complete relaxation. One lets the mind and the body go and resolves to do nothing. Sitting quietly in erect posture, one resolves to abandon all effort and allows calmness and silence to settle in all parts of being. A basic presupposition of the conception of meditation is that God dwells in the heart of every individual. The light of truth steadily shines in the depth of each soul. When absolute silence reigns supreme, the indwelling

* Haridas Chaudhuri, *Integral Yoga* (London: George Allen & Unwin Ltd., 1965), pp. 118-29.

truth shines out. One begins to see things exactly as they are. The truth about oneself and about one's environment clearly emerges in the field of consciousness.

It should be noted here that the meditational technique of relaxation is radically different from that of sleep. In sleep the conscious mind is submerged in the unconscious. The rational will is put out of action. The idea is to give maximum rest to the whole body and the nervous system. But in the meditational method of relaxation, the idea is to establish conscious communion with the depths of the unconscious. It is to unify the whole personality, breaking down all barriers and divisions within it. The conscious mind becomes utterly receptive to the inner light. It is reduced to emptiness so that it may reverberate with the wordless sound of Silence. In religious terminology, the conscious falls quiet so that the power of God may be overtly operative in one's whole being.

Whereas sleep is induced by instinct, meditational relaxation is throughout guided by intelligence. One lets go the mind and the body and at the same time adopts the attitude of a detached onlooker. The meditator's attitude is like that of an expert snake charmer who brings his snake out into the open from his basket and lets it go so that it can freely move around. But he keeps a constant, vigilant watch upon it. Similarly the meditator lets the snake of his mind loose, allows it to act freely without interference, but keeps a constant watch upon it. The meditator allows his thoughts, feelings, impulses, movements, to pass like a flock of birds across his mental firmament. He just observes them. He tries to analyze and understand them. He allows free movement to all his psychic contents, whether good or bad, right or wrong. He refuses to be carried off by any wave of emotion or wind of fantasy. If, in an unguarded moment, he is so carried off and finds himself in the realm of fantasy, he immediately shakes himself free and resumes his position of a detached onlooker. As long-forgotten memories, suppressed wishes, unspoken emotions, march past his observation post, he carefully takes note of them all. He also takes note of his instinctive emotional reactions and value judgments in regard to them. Extending to them the same attitude of objective observation, he disentangles himself from the flux of instinct, emotions, and the like.

As he proceeds in this way, following the method of self-transcending awareness, he becomes, at one stage, aware of himself as an observer. He cognizes his own ego and makes it into an object. He perceives how other people think of him and how God may think of him. He moves in the direction of egoless consciousness. As he does so, a power much greater than his own becomes active within him. It is his own hitherto dormant central power. It may be called the latent power of God within him. With the awakening of the central psychic energy, meditation becomes an effortless and spontaneous affair. The meditator as an individual finds himself caught up in a unifying and self-transcending movement of consciousness. There is maximum intensification of consciousness regulated from the deepest center of personality. This is accompanied by an ever-deepening experience of peace, power, joy and love. The final goal of the self-transcending and self-integrating movement of consciousness is the discovery of the nontemporal dimension of existence. Here the individual finds himself at one with the totality of being. It is the existential experience of what religion calls God.

As one can easily notice here, meditational relaxation

involves a high degree of indrawn concentration. Concentration on any external object is replaced here by concentration upon one's mental flux. It assumes the form of phenomenological observation of the whole psyche. No ethico-religious judgment, no practical motivation, no utilitarian motive, no metaphysical concern with the real and the unreal, is allowed to interfere with such observation. But in the practice of meditation, such phenomenological observation is intended to serve a final purpose. The goal of such inward observation is thorough acquaintance with one's own personality including its assets and liabilities, virtues and shortcomings, its deepest desires and aspirations. In the course of meditation one acquires emotional tolerance for the shadow side of personality, including one's foibles and frailties. One begins to organize one's fundamental wishes and aspirations in an intelligent manner. Out of such self-organization and self-integration is born the transcendental awareness of the ultimate ground of existence. Such awareness opens the hidden springs of creative inspiration, shedding light upon the ultimate meaning of life.

Phenomenological self-observation is motivated by pure theoretical interest. It aims at a theoretical investigation of the psyche in all its manifestations. But the kind of self-observation involved in the practice of meditation is purposive and existential. It is prompted by the existential passion to become what one essentially is. It is guided by the will to live in harmony with the fundamental truth of existence. The passion to be, the will to live in the light of Being, is the essential structure of human reality. From the standpoint of meditation, the intellectual act of phenomenological self-observation is only a subordinate factor in existential self-fulfillment.

But is not the method of detached self-observation an acceptance of the principle of dualism? Is not ultimate reality nondual and undivided? By adopting the attitude of a transcendent onlooker, is not the meditator introducing radical division right within his own existence? Is not meditation disruptive of the unitary functioning of personality?

In answer to such doubts or objections, it must be remembered that the gateway to the vision of the nondual truth lies through a sharp awareness of differences as they are. Reality is nondual—but not in the sense that such differences as instinct and reason, matter and form, emotion and knowledge, memory and anticipation, perception and hallucination, theory and fact, symbol and symbolized, subject and object are all unreal. The truth is the exact opposite. Such differences are vitally real. The proper understanding of such differences is the essence of wisdom. Reality is nondual in the sense that such differences, in spite of their sharp distinctiveness, are not existentially separate or discontinuous. In truth, they are closely interrelated and inseparably associated aspects of the one continuum of Being.

The purpose of meditation is not to regress to the impulsive behavior pattern of the child or the primitive. It is not to regress to the spontaneity of the animal instinct. That would be the negation of centuries of cultural development and ethico-religious progress registered in the march of civilization. The purpose of meditation is to discover that ultimate ground of existence in which all differences are reconciled without losing their distinctive character. It aims at that ultimate principle of unity from which endless differences flow in their colorful richness. It aims at that kind of self-integration in which actions are prompted not by unthinking impulse or arbitrary caprice, but by luminous vision of the cosmic purpose of one's individual existence.

The light of wisdom born of meditation is like the non-discriminating light of the sun. It shines equally upon all without any bias and prejudice. But precisely in so doing, it reveals all differences exactly as they are as the richly diversified expression of the One. In consequence, the wise man's life is on the one hand uniquely colorful. On the other it is directed to the welfare of all.

(5) *Discernment and Critical Evaluation.* Concentration and detached self-observation do not exhaust the meaning of meditation as spiritual practice (*dhyāna*). Meditation is incomplete without growing spiritual discernment and critical evaluation (*viveka*).

Concentration is, to be sure, an important aspect of meditation. It enhances one's mental power and increases one's efficiency. It may even lead to the unfolding of such powers of extrasensory perception as clairvoyance, clairaudience, telepathy, etc. But with all his power, efficiency, and paranormal ability a person may choose to serve the demon instead of the divine. He may yield to the temptation of using power for self-aggrandizement instead of social progress. In such a case, concentration ceases to be an ingredient of meditation proper. It rather degenerates into intensified ego pursuit.

Meditation is concentration plus a deepening sense of higher values. It is the increasing orientation of the concentrated mind toward union with Being as the source of all values.

Similarly, detached self-observation is practised in meditation not for its own sake, nor for the sake of mere relief from the strains and stresses of daily life. The latter is, of course, a gain of no mean importance. But there is much more to meditation proper. Meditation is the practice of detached self-observation, involving relaxation, self-emptying, etc., with a definite sense of direction and within the framework of a definite goal. That goal is the awareness of Being as the basis of all intrinsic values.

Since meditation is a search for intrinsic values as rooted in Being, the flame of discernment and critical evaluation has always to be kept alive in the mind. As deeper powers emerge, the temptation to employ them for selfish purposes must be subdued. As colorful visions enchant the mind, the tendency to be carried away must be curbed.

Sometimes one may experience rapturous ecstasies and mistake them for *nirvāna* or enlightenment. Many young people nowadays are making this mistake under the influence of various potent drugs. But one must remember that enlightenment which is the goal of meditation is not a mere subjective experience of delightful ecstasy, however exciting. True enlightenment is the unclouded awareness of Being. Awareness of Being is, no doubt, accompanied by an experience of profound delight. But not all delightful experiences amount to the authentic awareness of Being.

While engaged in meditation one may sometimes have the heavenly experience of beholding graceful gods and goddesses. But one must remember that they are nothing but projections of one's unconscious mind conditioned by good karma. Other times one may have the hellish experience of being tormented by terrifying monsters and demons. Here also one must remember that these dark forces are nothing but projections of one's own unconscious mind, conditioned by bad karma. Such discernment and evaluation would help maintain one's calm self-poise and blissful rootedness in Being. Being is beyond the duality of gods and demons, beyond both angels and monsters. Awareness of Being is penetrative insight into the creative ground of all things and living creatures. It is luminous apprehension of the oneness of all existence as the diversified expression of Being.

(6) *Enlightenment.* Meditation is authenticated with the attainment of enlightenment. Without enlightenment it is reduced to an exercise in futility. A man may spend his whole life practising yogic postures, breathing exercises, and various lessons in concentration. But in the absence of illumination, he misses the most important thing about meditation.

Enlightenment, which is the soul of meditation, is the awareness of Being. Corresponding to the four fundamental dimensions of Being, it may be said that enlightenment is fourfold.

First, enlightenment is the awareness of Being as the formless ground of all existence, as timeless transcendence. In this respect it is transcendental consciousness, a profound experience of the peace that passeth understanding.

Secondly, enlightenment is the awareness of Being manifest as the cosmic whole. It is a beatific vision of the universe in its total unity. From this perspective, all of life is accepted as it is, and appreciated in its overruling harmony and beauty.

Thirdly, enlightenment is the awareness of Being perpetually self-expressive as the evolutionary movement of time. In consequence, it is a concerned recognition of life as a task—the task to participate in the being of the world and to carry evolution to ever-new heights of glory. In the Bhagavadgītā, Chapter XI, Lord Krishna unfolds to Arjuna this awe-inspiring vision of all-originating and all-absorbing Time, and urges him to act.

Fourthly, enlightenment is the awareness of Being as the self (*ātman*), as the inmost center of one's own existence. It is the experience of freedom and self-sufficiency. It is the discovery of the divine within oneself. Such self-knowledge marks the full flowering of one's personality.

(7) *Dedication to Cosmic Welfare.* We are now ready to understand the final phase of meditation. It consists in active dedication to cosmic welfare. While meditation in its essence is the awareness of Being, meditation in its fruit is the service of Being in the fullness of love.

Medieval mystics both in India and in Europe frequently equated enlightenment with transcendental consciousness, i.e., awareness of Being as eternal peace or supernal bliss. This has an irresistible fascination for all those who are weary of life or disenchanted with society. Those who find life-in-this-world meaningless are inclined to magnify transcendental consciousness as the acme of wisdom.

But transcendental consciousness is the awareness of only one aspect of Being, namely, its timeless transcendence. Being is also, as we have seen, the cosmic whole, the evolutionary movement of time, and the individual self as a unique creative center. Unified awareness of Being in its multiform fullness makes enlightenment a creative act. It assumes the form of dedication to cosmic welfare.

By virtue of total enlightenment an individual experiences transcendent peace within himself and at the same time resolves to offer his best for the good of all. Inward illumination spontaneously issues forth into altruistic action.

Meditation as the art of gaining total enlightenment is thus integrative and dynamic. It flowers into thoroughly integrated awareness of Being in its fullness. It obtains fruition in free, spontaneous, and joyful self-expression, in a spirit of dedication to the collective good of man (*janahita*).

CHAPTER X

The Problem of Identity

THE PROBLEM OF IDENTITY lies at the very center of human existence. A multitude of other problems stem from it.

Every individual self is a unique whole of content, a distinct personality. He has his roots in a particular socio-cultural soil. He draws his nourishment from that soil. He grows and matures in a particular historical context from which he unconsciously imbibes his ideas and norms, his hopes and aspirations. Is he aware of his invisible vital link to the historical matrix of existence?

Every individual has an intrinsic value and a unique importance of his own. He is capable of making a unique contribution to the world. If he is actively aware of this fact, his life becomes meaningful. It moves forward as a creative process of growth and self-fulfillment. Whereas in the absence of such awareness all sense of value and meaning is lost. Life is reduced to a nightmare, to a "tale told by an idiot full of sound of fury signifying nothing."

The problems of most crucial importance in a person's life are reflected in such questions as: "Who am I?" "Where have I come from?" "Where am I going?" "Where do I stand in the universe?" Some kind of answer to these questions is essential for a man to live as a human being. Such questions are vital factors in his search for meaning. When he discovers an answer to these within himself, a magic transformation of personality is likely to take place. Unsuspected capabilities are released. Hidden springs of creativity are opened. A clear sense of direction is acquired. A firm basis of decision is attained. And in consequence life becomes creatively meaningful. An authentic sense of identity thus opens the door to the most treasured spiritual gains. In the contrary case, loss of identity disintegrates life. Not even the conquest of the whole world can completely make up for that abysmal loss. "What shall it avail thee if thou gaineth the whole world and loseth thine own soul?"

Loss of identity has been described in ancient scriptures as loss of contact with one's own soul. It is self-oblivion, or self-forgetfulness of one's authentic self. In modern phraseology, it is self-alienation or estrangement from one's inmost center of being. It is the loss of substance, the shattering of existence. It is the feeling of being uprooted from one's own spiritual soil.

Every crucial stage in the growth of personality is characterized by the death of the old self and the birth of a new one. At the beginning of every new phase of higher development, a person asks himself the question with a new sense of urgency: "Who am I?" The raising of this question already reflects the inkling of a new identity, of a deeper and more authentic aspect of the self.

There was a man who was faced with a great problem every morning when he got up from bed. He would forget where he had placed his trousers and his coat. On finding them he would have to look for his tie and his hat. And then for his pen and his watch. The problem became so acute, that he was afraid of going to bed at night. But one night he hit upon a bright idea. On a piece of paper he wrote down, in a definite order, different items of his outfit kept at specified places. Next morning he woke up a new man. He took that piece of paper and knew exactly where the different things were. But as soon as he was dressed and ready to go out, an unexpected new problem suddenly presented itself. That morning the new question that strangely entered his mind was: "Where am I?—Where do I stand in this wide universe?" With the posing of this question, this habitually lethargic and forlorn man was on his way to a new life of creative joy and meaningful action.

The problem of identity can be discussed from different standpoints: psychological, socio-political, ethical, metaphysical, and spiritual. We shall briefly indicate in this chapter the specific nature of these different aspects of the problem.

THE PSYCHOLOGICAL ASPECT

Psychologically speaking, an individual's sense of identity is the offshoot of his identification with different significant individuals early in life. In a healthy family of emotionally mature parents, the growing male child will more and more identify himself with his father. The image of the father will be a determining factor in his expanding vision of the future. He will increasingly imbibe in a greater or lesser measure the values and ideals of the father. As he keeps growing up, his ego-ideal evolves through his identification with such father-surrogates as the teacher in school, the professor in college, the religious prophet, the political leader, and so forth. In his relationship to the mother, he develops the attitude of emotional loyalty, not existential identification. He feels proud of himself as the son of such an affectionate and self-effacing mother. He loves and respects his mother. But he does not want to be like his mother and play a feminine role in life by relinquishing his masculine traits. On the other hand a growing female child would more and more identify herself existentially with her mother. She would develop her sense of identity as a loving and beautiful female. But in her relationship to her father, she would develop the attitude of affection, respect, and loyalty. She would grow with the spirit of obedience and submission to the father and respect for all that the father stands for. But she would not want to become like the father, adopting his masculine role.

Let us now consider a different family setup. The growing male child has not much contact with the father, who may be habitually away from home, lacking interest in his family, an alcoholic, an imbecile, or just too aloof and self-centered. Consequently the boy, as he grows up, develops an existential identification with the mother. The mother enters into his psyche as the determinant of his self-image. So he develops an effeminate attitude toward life. He may become a homosexual, finding delight in displaying feminine qualities and virtues. Similarly, the growing female child may establish an identification with the father. If the mother's position in the family is, for some reason or other, contemptible or deplorable, or if deep down she feels that the feminine role is a contemptible one, the girl may begin to play a tomboy, and adopt the masculine self-image.

We may now consider a still different state of affairs.

The atmosphere of the family may be extremely confused and bewildered. Parents may suffer from extreme emotional instability, neither of them capable of projecting any clear and definite image. Sometimes it is the father who lavishes the affection—excessive and unusual affection—upon the child. He is perhaps using the child as a means of personal security or self-importance. But it may not take long for the situation to change abruptly and unexpectedly. He may become suddenly aloof and strangely indifferent to the child. Or he may start scolding the child or punishing him for no apparent reason. He is just giving vent to his anger and his resentment against his spouse. The result is that the child is left utterly confused. The same thing happens in his relationship to the mother. Sometimes she is extremely sweet and indulgent, bubbling over with motherly affection. But it is unpredictable: suddenly she may turn into the opposite and begin to behave like a witch. These whimsically fluctuating moods of the parents appear completely unrelated to any objective cause. Under such circumstances the growing child has no opportunity of developing any firm identification. He grows up with a confused and bewildered mind. He feels that he does not know who he is and where he stands. In the absence of any sense of identity, he fails to acquire any guiding principle of life. He does not know on what basis to make decisions in the sphere of action.

Lack of identity is an intolerable psychic condition. It threatens to paralyze the whole being. No wonder that in such a situation an individual is driven to grasp any identity or identifying label he can conveniently lay his hands upon.

A child who is unwanted in the family or who is constantly scolded and criticized is deprived of any opportunity for identity-formation in the home. So he picks up his identification from the outside world. A rejection in the home provides him with the broad outline of his self-image. He is good-for-nothing, he is evil, he is a scum. Endowed with such a vaguely negative image about himself, he is likely to gravitate to the company of others who similarly feel neglected by society. He swells the ranks of juvenile delinquents. In their company his identity blank is more and more concretely filled, albeit in a negative fashion. He begins to accept his identity as a rebel, as a cheated, neglected, and rejected one who owes it to himself and to his associates to destroy the society that has maltreated him.

Since a man cannot live without a sense of identity, an opprobrious or condemned identity is naturally preferred to no identity. This has been brought out with remarkable clarity in Jean-Paul Sartre's book *Saint Genet*. Jean Genet is the celebrated French criminal-poet-playwright. He never knew his own parents and was raised by strangers. In early childhood he gets into the habit of stealing all kinds of things. Stolen objects which he can call his own seem to provide him with some sort of basis for identity. The more he steals and accumulates things, the more this basis is strengthened. One day at the age of ten he is caught, and society brands him as a thief. He is condemned, but at the same time saved. He now discovers a determinate identity in the appellation "thief." Henceforth he must carry on thievery as his personal destiny. It is fascinating to see how, in carrying out his identity as a thief, he undergoes further transformations of personality as a saint of the underworld, as an existential hero, as a poet, playwright, actor, and martyr.*

* Jean-Paul Sartre, *Saint Genet* (New York: George Braziller, 1963).

It is evident, then, from the foregoing, that a healthy and emotionally stable family atmosphere is of paramount importance for the formation of the right kind of identity in growing children.

THE ETHICAL ASPECT

From the ethical standpoint, every mode of identity has some value or disvalue attached to it. There are some duties, responsibilities, and privileges attached to every socially accepted identity. There are also priorities to be observed among different identities. The identity of a thief or a murderer or a kidnapper carries an ethical disvalue. As an operative principle it is disruptive of the social order. The identity of a police officer, a soldier, a judge, a teacher, or a lawyer is ethically valuable. It helps in maintaining law and order and in promoting social progress.

There are different types of identity: family identity, communal identity, racial identity, religious identity, political identity, and so on. An individual comes from such and such a family. He is a member of a particular country. He belongs to a particular race and religion. He is a citizen of a particular state; maybe he is active in a particular political party. These different identities impose upon him different obligations and also confer upon him various rights and privileges. Each identity carries a well-defined set of functions and activities. When, for instance, a policeman acts in conformity with the socio-ethical image of the police officer, captures a criminal when the opportunity arises and brings him to law, he is right and good. When he violates that image by accepting bribes, he is condemned and punished by society accordingly. Within each family, different members—father, mother, son, daughter, brother, sister—have their more or less well-defined ethical rights and duties.

The most fundamental ethical issue is the question of priority among the different identities of an individual. A person suspected of committing theft or murder is brought to trial in a criminal court. The judge happens to be a friend of the suspected person's family. Can the judge allow his friendship to prejudice him in favor of the criminal? Or, should he firmly set aside such considerations and function in his identity as the custodian of justice and public welfare? The verdict of conscience is clear in emphasizing the priority of the latter identity.

A certain individual happens to be a very loyal and active member of a political party in a particular nation. But besides being a party member he belongs to the nation as a citizen. Ethical considerations would unequivocally place his national identity above his party identity. The party is there to serve the best interests of the nation. Its power drive should not be carried to such an extent as to injure the large national interest. When there is a serious clash between the party and the nation, there should be no doubt in the mind of the individual as to the priority of his national identity.

Racism or racial prejudice is ethically reprehensible because it places racial identity above humanity. There are different races in the world. There are peoples with different colors of skin—white, black, brown, yellow, and whatever other shades of color there may be. It is natural for each race to have its own pride. It is natural for each to endeavor to maintain its own continuity and distinctive character. But when this racial consciousness is carried to such an extent as to encourage violent hatred against other races, it becomes a crime against humanity. When racism releases its destructive fury against foreigners with a different pigmentation of the skin, the sense of identity suffers a vicious corruption. Over and above their racial identities, all peoples are basically human beings. Their identity as man has precedence over racial or communal affiliation.

For similar reasons, religious sectarianism or parochialism is ethically reprehensible. Over and above the fact of belonging to different religions, man is man. His identity as a human being is superior to his identity as a Christian or a Buddhist or a Hindu or a Moslem or a Jew. If his religious beliefs and activities encourage him to commit a crime against humanity, it is high time to do some critical thinking about his superstitious religious ideas.

The ethical problem can also be stated in another way. What is man's best identity with respect to his psycho-social structure? Is he an absolutely independent, self-contained individual? Is he a cell of the social organism? Or has he an independent dimension of existence besides his status as a responsible member of the social order? Individualism, socialism, and integralism provide different answers to these questions.*

One may again inquire: is man essentially pleasure-seeking, or is he essentially a rational creature, impulse being an adventitious impurity of his nature? Or is he a supernatural entity imprisoned in the flesh due to his fall from the grace of God? Or is he a multidimensional being with physical, mental, moral and nontemporal dimensions of existence, entrusted with the task of

* For a brief discussion of this problem, see my *Sri Aurobindo: The Prophet of Life Divine*, 2nd ed. (Pondicherry: Sri Aurobindo Ashram, 1960), pp. 184-90.

achieving a dynamic harmony of them all? A proper understanding of his essential identity would be the key to all his other problems. Hedonism, rationalism, supernaturalism, and integralism seek to define man's inmost identity in different ways. According to integral nondualism, an individual is, on the one hand, a constituent element of the social structure. According to his talent and unique potentiality, he has to find his proper place and function therein. He rightfully enjoys the benefits of social existence and civilization, and is called upon to make his own contribution to society in the best way he can. On the other hand, he has a mode of existence entirely outside of the social order. With that mode of existence, he stands alone in his relationship with the Alone. He discovers his deepest allegiance and most profound responsibility in this sphere. The gradual sharpening of his insight with regard to the precise nature of this allegiance and responsibility is a matter of his progressive inward evolution.

THE METAPHYSICAL ASPECT

From the metaphysical standpoint, the problem of identity is concerned with the precise nature of that principle which confers continuity and identity upon human existence. Every human being is what he is. Socrates is Socrates, and Plato is Plato. Buddha is Buddha and Christ is Christ. Of course, every individual is also constantly changing, from day to day, from month to month, from year to year. Changes in bodily existence, in social relationships, in ideas, feelings, imaginings, experiences, desires, plans, are sometimes very slow and imperceptible. But sometimes again they are abrupt, radical, revolutionary, altering the individual almost beyond recognition. Despite all these continuous changes of varying proportions, an individual remains one identical individual. From birth to death, every individual, whether Socrates or Plato, or Buddha or Christ —or some anonymous unit of the vast multitude—has one continuous and identical life. No amount of change can turn Paul into Peter, Plato into Socrates, or the Buddha into Christ. No amount of change can substantially transform one man into another. Why not? What is the exact nature of this principle of continuity and identity?

Traditional metaphysics holds that every identical individual is in respect of his inmost identity an unchanging and unchangeable spiritual substance. He is a soul, essentially different from all other souls, holding his own against all extraneous changes. Similarly, the identity of a material substance, say a table, consists in the presence of an unchanging material substance to which the distinctive qualities of the object belong. This underlying substance is a mysterious, unknown factor, an indeterminable "X." Whatever is determinately known is a determination, a quality, an attribute, or a sense datum or perceptum.

Now in modern thought the old metaphysical notion has been rejected. Substance as an unknown and unknowable "X" is worthless as a principle of explanation. Known facts and phenomena can hardly be explained in terms of the unknown. Moreover, substance as an unchanging entity is an entirely trans-empirical concept. All entities we know, all objects and events, are like blocks of change. Nothing that we experience falls outside of the law of change.

As a result of rejecting the unknown as a principle of explanation, we find that in modern science the notion of substance has been replaced by the notion of energy. A material object is not a mass of changing qualities belonging to an unchanging substance. It is a configuration of measurable energy units or energy vibrations. It is an organized system of changes. Its identity resides not in the mystery of any unchanging substance but in the continuity of a certain pattern of configuration.

Similarly the identity of a human individual lies not in any mysterious unknown and unknowable, unchanging and unchangeable, soul substance. No amount of introspection or honest self-inquiry discloses any such mysterious entity. Just as in physical science substance has been replaced by energy, so also in modern psychology the old metaphysical concept of a permanent mental substance has been replaced by the notion of psychic energy or libido.

The human individual is identical insofar as he is a determinate mind-body continuum. In the course of his constant change and maturation he preserves a certain pattern. He is a specific constellation of physical and mental processes. His identity is like that of a song or a piece of music. It is like that of a burning flame or a flowing stream. But what about the individual's consciousness which becomes aware of his existence as a stream or as a piece of music? Is it not outside the flux of change which it cognizes? Certainly it is. In cognizing change consciousness transcends change. In apprehending the continuous movement of time, consciousness undoubtedly transcends time. But consciousness is no thing, no object. It is neither change nor substance, both of which are its objective contents. Consciousness is, to use a Buddhist expression, Emptiness (Śunyatā). It is, as Sartre points out, Nothingness. It is, as Vedānta puts it, indeterminable Being.

But consciousness as Nothingness is still recognizable as a function which transcends both body and mind, both the physical and the psychical series. It is an emergent value. It emerges at the human stage of evolution. It is the mode in which pure transcendence operates in human life.

Consciousness reveals the distinctive potential of a human individual. In consequence, it confers upon the individual a sense of destiny, a sense of his unique avocation. This lifts the identity of an individual into a higher plane. An individual aware of his unique potential enjoys an exalted sense of identity. His identity is qualitatively different from that of a rock or a plant or an animal, or even of the average anonymous man who follows the crowd.

THE SPIRITUAL ASPECT

The foregoing discussion leads us right to the heart of the spiritual problem of identity.

What is the identity of the individual in his relationship to ultimate reaelity? How does the human individual stand related to God or the absolute? Discovery of this relationship alone can help him live in the light of the supreme truth. There can be no salvation or liberation without such discovery. Ultimate self-fulfillment can ensue only upon the realization of one's authentic spiritual identity.

Much of traditional religious and mystical thinking interprets the spirit in man in supernaturalistic or transcendentalist terms. Supernaturalism affirms the reality of a supernatural kingdom of heaven beyond the uttermost limits of the natural order. The supernatural alone is ultimately real. The human individual as a spir-

itual entity belongs in essence to the supernatural kingdom. His bondage and suffering consist in his fall from
the supernatural due to his sinfulness. His existence in
the realm of matter is a kind of exile; it is a fall from
grace. It is punishment for his sins. His ultimate goal is
complete dissociation—emancipation from the fetters of
the flesh—and rehabilitation in the spiritual kingdom of
heaven. On this view, then, the human individual in his
spiritual essence has a separate, exalted mode of existence apart from the natural order. He is a kind of substance radically different from material substance.

Traditional mysticism, insofar as it goes beyond religious supernaturalism, envisages man's spiritual identity
in transcendentalist terms. The spirit in man is not a
separate substance, ethereal, supernatural, or otherwise.
All substances are, in ultimate analysis, spacio-temporal
configurations. They exist in space, whether natural or
supernatural space. They endure in time, whether physical or mental time. Consequently spirit is beyond substance and attribute, quantity and quality. It is a
radically different dimension of existence altogether. It
is not a reality outside the natural order, not a kingdom
outside the realm of matter. As the spaceless and timeless dimension of existence, the spirit pervades the entire natural order and sustains the realm of matter. The
spirit in man is the element of pure transcendence in
him. To know the spirit is to comprehend the oneness
of all existence, and to realize man's essential identity
with the Supreme Being. So the highest and profoundest
mystical realization is summed up in the dictum: "That
art Thou." The human individual in his inmost self is
identical with the Supreme, in the same way as finite
space, enclosed in a room, is one with infinite space.

Supernaturalism is the popular objectivized version

of mysticism. It fosters other-worldliness. It drives a wedge between nature and supernature, and posits an ontological division in the heart of reality.

Mysticism deals with the pure spiritual dimension of man, his nontemporal dimension. It reveals Being as the all-comprehensive medium of existence in which all opposites such as one and many, individual and universal, change and permanence, are reconciled. But exclusive preoccupation with the nontemporal produces indifference to the world. It makes the mystic apathetic to the social, economical, and political values of existence. It blocks appreciation of the intrinsic value and significance of space and time, of evolution and individuation.

The total truth about the spiritual identity of man can be disclosed only in a unified outlook in which naturalism and mysticism, evolutionism and eternalism, are properly reconciled.

The human individual, in his spiritual essence, is a unique synthesis of the natural and the spiritual. He represents a dynamic emergent value. On the natural side, he is a highly differentiated mind-body continuum. He is endowed with a nervous system so highly developed that it is capable of reflecting the light of the nontemporal. On the spiritual side, he is a unique focus of the nontemporal. He is a child of immortality. As the material and the spiritual, the temporal and the nontemporal, meet in him, he becomes endowed with such emergent characteristics as consciousness, freedom, value sense, and ego-transcendence. He develops such emergent qualities as love, devotion to truth, and genuine concern for cosmic welfare.

On the natural side, man belongs to the cosmic whole. He belongs to a family, to a community, to a race, to a nation, to the international order. In the last analysis, he belongs to the evolutionary world-spirit—to the evolutionary whole of nature.

On the purely spiritual side, man has a mode of existence beyond all groupings and collectivities. He has a mode of existence beyond change and evolution, beyond birth, growth, decay and death. In that mode he is pure freedom and joy. No fear and anxiety, no doubt and despair, can affect him there. But the distinction of the natural and the spiritual does not denote any division in the heart of man. They are not two types of substance of which man is composed. They are two inseparable aspects or dimensions of the same reality that the human individual is. As a synthesis of time and eternity, man's higher function is to participate in the creative flow of time with that fearless self-poise and serenity which is born of union with the eternal.

One may look at the essential structure of man from any one of these opposite standpoints. Viewed from the natural standpoint, man is a child of evolutionary Nature, capable of carrying evolution to higher levels of creation. Viewed from the spiritual standpoint, man is a child of the immortal spirit, precipitated into the evolutionary march of time. His dynamic sense of higher values is rooted in this fact.

CHAPTER XI

How to Live a Balanced Life

TRUTH IS HARMONY. It is that unified whole of existence in which all apparent contradictions are reconciled. It is also that self-coherent vision of existence in which all fragmentary viewpoints are harmonized.

It follows that true life is harmonious self-development in response to total reality. It is the balanced growth of personality with a view to serving the cosmic purpose of life.

There can be no abiding happiness without balanced growth. The lasting joy of fulfillment can spring only from the integration of one's total personality. Exclusive satisfaction of this or that particular aspect of life such as a passing impulse or an isolated desire can produce pleasure, but not abiding happiness. True happiness is a function of one's total desire-nature organized into a self-coherent whole.

There are many conflicting tendencies in our human nature. There are all too many conflicting impulses and motivations. A grievous mistake frequently made is to push this or that particular desire too far. An attempt is often made to solve the inner conflict by pursuing the policy of extremism, that is to say, by exaggerating the importance of one aspect of life at the cost of all others.

A successful businessman, drunk with the wine of success, may develop a one-track mind. In his all-consuming passion for mounting success in business, he sets aside all other activities. He turns a blind eye to all other interests in life, and smothers the promptings of his inner soul. The growing millions in his bank balance seem to compensate him for all other lapses and failures. Dishonest practices and unscrupulous deals are justified as a necessary evil. Increasing disengagement from family life and apathy toward cultural and spiritual values may appear as the natural price to be paid or the necessary sacrifice to be made at the altar of the god of success.

But at the very peak of his glamorous career as a millionaire business executive, he may one day suddenly feel his life inwardly impoverished. A look into the abyss within himself scares him to death. A gripping sense of inner emptiness gnaws at his heart. After the actual accumulation of desired millions, what next? What is the value of it all? The prospect of one day having to leave all the amassed millions behind, robs them of their intrinsic value. A retrospective glance at the suppression of finer emotions and the sacrifice of higher values fills the mind with repentance and despair. In other words, the one-track pursuit of an isolated goal more often than not leads to a dead end. At the end of the mad rush, one finds gold turning into ashes, success into sorrow.

If extremism in the service of Mammon is a vice, extremism in the service of God is a grievous error. Those who prematurely renounce life and turn their backs on society with the idea of finding God, act neurotically. They delude themselves and justify their actions with high-sounding, nebulous concepts. They try to run away from their problems, but inescapably carry the problems on their backs, wherever they run. By suppressing natural desire, they accumulate nervous tension. By having to fight constantly with the demonic forces threatening from their hide-outs in the unconscious mind, they dissipate vast amounts of energy and create emotional blocks in the unconscious mind. In point of truth, extremism in the quest of God reduces God to an extreme opposite of life. Such an extreme God ceases to be God. Far from being the opposite of life, God, truly understood, is the harmonizing principle of life. God is that in whom the antithetical aspects of life are reconciled, the multitudinous desires of one's nature are harmoniously fulfilled. So the authentic search for God is the search for balanced and harmonious living. It is not a movement away from life.

Sri Aurobindo, the great sage of Pondicherry, has warned that the premature pulling in of the power of God may prove disastrous. Contact with the Divine is an overwhelming experience. It contains terrific power. If high power descends upon the body when it is not yet ready and sufficiently strong, mental derangement may ensue. Some people are so much carried off by emotional waves flowing from the impact, that they squander much precious energy through erratic behavior such as wild dancing, singing, crying, or rolling on the floor. Sufficient preparation of mind and body, sufficient strengthening of the nervous system, and stability of emotion, must precede direct mystical experience. Balance is indeed the keynote of proper spiritual growth.

Introversion and extroversion are two opposite tendencies of the human mind. They represent two antithetical movements of consciousness. Whereas extroversion is the outgoing, other-loving movement of consciousness, introversion is the ingoing, self-loving movement of consciousness. Extroversion is the mind's orientation to the objective; introversion is the mind's orientation to the subjective. Introversion and extroversion are present in varying proportions in different individuals. Those who are predominantly extroverted believe that all the good things of life come from outside. So they become acquisitive and aggressive. They love to meet people and go to parties. They like to be surrounded with all kinds of precious things. They like to be engaged in all kinds of affairs. Mingling with the march of events in the outside world is their style of living.

Those who are predominantly introverted believe that all the good things of life come from within. So they more and more withdraw into the private world of their subjective existence. They believe that the outside world is only a shadow cast by the creative spirit that dwells within. So they tread the lonely path of detachment. Exploration of the inner realm of consciousness is their thrilling pastime. All-out adventure in the domain of spirit is their style of living.

A person who is too much of an extrovert leads a superficial life. A gripping feeling of inward emptiness gradually eats into his vitals. In spite of all his impressive outward possessions, he may suffer from an unaccountable sense of frustration. A feeling of alienation from the center of his being may undermine the whole glittering superstructure of his outward accomplishments.

On the other hand, a person who is too much of an introvert leads a mutilated life. He suppresses an essential part of his personality, namely, relatedness to the outside world and to fellow beings. No individual can develop his full potential except through interpersonal relations and through a continuous dialogue with others. Participation in social evoluton is an essential ingredient of self-development and personal fulfillment. As an introvert withdraws more and more into his private world, he experiences a sense of alienation from the social environment. He begins to feel himself a stranger in this world. Having failed in social adjustment, he curses society as incorrigibly evil or as a deceptive shadow-show. Bitterness mingles with loneliness in his inward being.

A perfect man is one who succeeds in bringing together, in harmonious balance, the extroverted and introverted tendencies of his nature. Korzybski once rightly observed that a perfect man is either an introverted extrovert or an extroverted introvert.* If a person happens to be mainly an introvert, let him constructively follow the bent of his own nature. Let him gain increasing insight into his inner self, into the vast regions of the unconscious psyche, and into his relationship to the eternal. According to his natural line of interest, let him gather treasures in art, psychology, religion, or mysticism. But, at the same time, let all his introverted pursuits be controlled by the motivation of serving society and humanity. Let him remember that ultimate reality is not the self, but the self-society continuum. The ultimate truth is not the spirit, but the spirit-nature continuum. The absolute is not an extracosmic God, but the God-world continuum. So self-exploration must be accompanied by increasing self-relatedness to the universe.

If a person happens to be mainly an extrovert, let him develop himself by following the bent of his own na-

* Alfred Korzybski, *Science and Sanity*, 4th ed. (Clinton, Mass.: The International Non-Aristotelian Library Publishing Co., 1962), p. 88.

ture. Let him acquire proficiency in such extroverted pursuits as sports, politics, trade and commerce, or business administration. But, at the same time, let him remember that there can be no ultimate happiness in life without due acknowledgement of the inner requirements of the soul. It would be good for him to cultivate some interest in aesthetic pursuits such as music, the dance, poetry, or painting. This should be treated as an area of life into which one can pour himself out of sheer love, setting aside all extraneous considerations of utility and profit. There should be some people in his life whom he can love just for the sake of love, setting aside all desires to dominate or exploit. There should be some moments in life in which he can leave the whole outside world behind him and enter into the perfect silence of his own being. These would be the moments of his quiet communion with himself—getting to know himself better, getting to know his relationship to the Supreme Creator. As he gains insight into himself, his extroverted pursuits would become more meaningful. They would acquire the new dimension of selfless social service and genuine dedication to human welfare. As through inward silence he would begin to experience the inward joy inherent in sheer existence, his outward activities would become a spontaneous outpouring of inner freedom.

INTELLIGENT SELF-ORGANIZATION

Intelligent self-organization is another fundamental principle of balanced living. There are a multitude of apparently conflicting desires interwoven in the human psyche. There are different instinctual drives such as appetite for food, sex, comfort, power, safety, and so forth. There are also purely rational sentiments, such as devotion to truth, striving for purity and perfection, sense of duty, ethical responsibility. Just as there are primitive egotistic impulses, there are also pure altruistic impulses such as sympathy, fellow-feeling, selfless love, spirit of sacrifice for the sake of others, and many more.

The basic dichotomy that runs right across the heart of human nature is what is traditionally described as flesh-and-spirit, passion-and-reason, impulse-and-law.

Some people strive in an uncompromising fashion to live a life of pure reason. They struggle to expunge from their nature what they call lower impulses and desires. They are rationalists, puritanists, and ascetics. They practice all manner of austerities and self-denying ordinances, in the interest of subjective purity and perfection. But in doing so they amputate a vital part of their nature, robbing life of its drive and dash, its spontaneity and creativity, its freshness and colorfulness. The unconscious psyche which is the abode of instinctual drives, is also the seat of creative energy. Suppression of the instinctual unconscious amounts, therefore, to a blocking of the springs of fresh creativity within oneself. It hinders the full flowering of personality. By producing inner conflicts and despair, it prevents the individual from reaching his true destiny, to wit, mature adulthood.

The instinctual drives are like horses that pull the chariot of the body. Reason is the check-rein. The individual is the driver. Instincts are, by nature, wild and chaotic. Once in a while they seem to become unmanageable. Puritanism represents a solution of the problem by cutting the instinctual horses loose from the chariot. In doing so, the individual may no doubt acquire some sort of mental peace. But it is the peace of the grave, not of life and victory. The fundamental task of life is not to cut out the horses, but to bring them under increasing control in order to travel toward the fulfillment of life's ultimate goal. The function of reason is not to destroy impulses but to channel them intelligently toward the higher ends of existence. An expert driver knows that horses can be trained and controlled with patience and understanding. When they are especially unruly, perhaps they are hungry or thirsty, perhaps fatigued or afraid, perhaps plagued by insects. When these disturbing factors are patiently and carefully removed, the wild animals behave with noble spirit.

Some people are extremely suspicious of reason and its discipline. They look upon all discipline as curtailment of natural liberty, wishing to live as they please in complete disregard of law and authority. Arbitrary whims and passing desires become their guiding light. They allow themselves to be led by the impulse of the moment. They are hedonists, epicureans, bohemians and beatniks. But the path of chaotic self-indulgence is no less self-defeating than that of ascetic self-denial. In vowing to serve freely the impulse of the moment, an individual becomes a slave of momentary impulses. His life is torn by conflicting desires. He drifts aimlessly, without purpose. Devoid of rhyme or reason, existence is reduced to a succession of convulsive movements. Pretty soon it is afflicted with a sense of nothingness or meaninglessness. Life acquires meaning only through self-transcendence. When a person succeeds in organizing his desires in the pursuit of some such transcendent goal as truth, beauty, social good, human welfare, liberation from bondage, or the brotherhood of man, life begins to make sense and boredom is overcome. But as soon as a commitment is made to some higher value, reason comes into play. One's impulses have now to submit to the discipline of reason in the service of the self-transcending cause.

So the secret of balanced life consists in realizing that passion and reason, flesh and spirit, are not irreconcilable aspects of human personality. One of them is not to be cut out in an attempt to glorify the other. Both of them, for all their apparent opposition, are indispensable and essential components of personality. Reason is there to organize passion. Passion is there to energize reason. The function of the indwelling spirit is to transform the flesh more and more into an image of the divine, into a temple of the eternal. The function of Nature is more and more to reflect the light of spirit in her bosom, to body forth the immaterial in the material.

The art of integrated living consists in the spirit of intelligent cooperation between nature and spirit. Nature is blind without spirit; spirit is lame without nature. According to a story in the Sānkhya philosophy of India, one time a blind man and a lame man got lost in a forest. Each by himself was in a helpless quandary. When they met each other, hope appeared. The lame man jumped upon the shoulders of the blind man. Together both could easily manage to get out of the forest and reach their destination. Similarly, nature and spirit —by virtue of their purposive togetherness—can together make life gloriously meaningful.

LAW OF BALANCED DISTRIBUTION

The fullest measure of happiness can be attained in life only by following the law of balanced distribution. Balanced distribution is an operative principle of the concept of harmony. It overrules all species of extremism and one-sided exaggeration. It organizes the different drives of personality in a balanced whole.

Suppose a man, at the end of a month's hard labor, receives his paycheck in the amount of $300. He may feel inclined to spend it in different ways. That very evening he may go to a wild party and squander all his money on champagne and gifts to girl friends. In that way he certainly buys one wonderful evening. But the rest of the month he finds himself broke and feels miserable. Exaggerated fulfillment of one particular need to the neglect of all other needs is the way of suffering, not of happiness. Maximum happiness demands a judicious distribution of one's earnings and available resources on the multitude of one's fundamental needs and aspirations.

So in harmonious living one has to take into account all the fundamental urges and aspirations of life. Life well lived is vital energy intelligently distributed among the various urges of life. Every individual has at his disposal a certain amount of energy. He can increase it within certain limits. He finds that there is an ebb and flow in the current of his life energy. It fluctuates from year to year. But all such fluctuations take place within certain limits. A mature person calculates how best he may distribute his available life energy among the most cherished objectives and projects of his life.

For instance, every normal individual has such basic

desires as comfortable living, freedom, loving companionship, spiritual longing in some form or other, and so
on. One may overemphasize one or two of the desires
and suppress the rest. The result of such overemphasis
would be apparently bubbling cheerfulness accompanied by a deep undercurrent of frustration in life. A
note of sadness born of self-suppression is bound to
vitiate the pleasures of imbalance. This applies not only
to the person who invests all his time in the gospel of
mammonism to the utter neglect of cultural and spiritual values. It also applies to the person who follows the
gospel of supernatural salvation by completely ignoring
social and material values.

BALANCED EDUCATION

Balanced education is essential for balanced living.
Lopsided intellectual development is a hindrance to
social welfare. It is also subversive of one's own happiness.

The keynote of balanced education is a judicious
combination of specialized training with the broadening
of outlook and human sympathies. A person who is a
jack-of-all-trades but master of none cannot make his
mark in life, especially in these days of specialization.
With ever-new frontiers opening in all branches of
knowledge and technology, the jack-of-all-trades type of
person has not much to contribute to social progress.
Moreover, without acquiring knowledge in depth in
some special area, a person becomes shallow. He can
move only on the periphery of life. He cannot operate
with authority in any field. He cannot speak with conviction. He develops no sense of rootedness in life.

We all know that in order to lift its head toward the

sky and spread its branches far and wide, a tree must be able to strike its roots deep in the soil. The deeper the root, the higher the shoot. Similarly, in order to be able to project himself into the advance of life and make any worth-while contribution, an individual must achieve specialized knowledge and skill in at least one area of life.

But at the same time over-specialization is another extreme to be avoided. It condemns life to a very narrow corner, closing all windows of communication with the ever-widening arena of human action and mutual relationship. A person with a one-track mind can easily become a devil's disciple: power born of specialized knowledge can bring about the most malignant inflation of the ego, and may prove dangerous to society.

True self-perfection consists in balanced self-development. According to his own specific talent, a man may decide to acquire specialized knowledge in a particular field. But at the same time he must develop a broad outlook on life, and broad human sympathies, as well as a broad understanding of the fundamental problems of the society in which he lives. It is only in the light of a broad humanistic outlook that he can make the most constructive and meaningful use of his specialized knowledge.

FIVE ASPECTS OF PERSONALITY

Broadly speaking, there are five aspects of human personality: physical, emotional, intellectual, moral, and spiritual. Self-perfection implies the harmonious development of all these aspects of existence.

There is no doubt that man is, in essence, a spiritual entity. But it is a grievous mistake to conceive of the spiritual as the direct antithesis of the physical. The traditional dichotomy of the flesh and the spirit is prompted by an inadequate grasp of the indivisible wholeness of life. The body is not a prison-house for the soul. Nor is it a mere ladder on which to climb up to the spirit so that, upon spiritual fulfillment, it can be kicked aside. On the contrary, the body is the façade of a temple in which the spirit dwells. Or, it may be described as the medium of creative self-expression of the spirit.

It follows that in balanced growth, the body has to be built up as a strong and fit instrument of higher living. It has to be purified and strengthened as a channel of divine action. It is sacrilegious to abuse the body, or to mortify the flesh in the name of God, or to mutilate the physical in a deluded effort to glorify the spiritual. On the other hand, the body is not to be pampered for its own sake. It is sheer stupidity to develop brawn at the cost of brain. It is foolish to follow the way of the flesh by turning a blind eye to life's higher values. The physical is to be strengthened as a means of pursuing higher values and realizing the eternal. It is also to be perfected as a medium of expressing the glory of the eternal in life and society.

The emotional is the most vital aspect of human personality. It embraces, on the one hand, the instinctual drives of nature. It includes, on the other, such fine sentiments as love of truth, compassion for others, devotion, and dedication. At the center of the emotional is the desire to love and to be loved. Without proper regulation and maturation of this love impulse, personality remains raw. A person may attain great intellectual eminence and yet emotionally remain a baby. For instance, a brilliant scholar may feel completely helpless away from his mother or his wife. He may become easily upset on hearing critical remarks about his scholarly achievements. A little flattery may induce him to form very superficial judgments about his flatterers, and prompt him to violate justice in his public behavior. He may be so wrapped up in the enchanted circle of his own ideas, that he becomes supremely indifferent to the sufferings of fellow beings. Genuine concern for others may be quite foreign to his inner makeup.

Emotional balance and maturity are essential ingredients of self-development. To this end one has to get closely acquainted with oneself. One has to be aware of the fundamental drives and desires of one's nature and fulfill them in an intelligent and organized fashion. One has to learn to relate to others meaningfully. Love is a two-way street. In order to receive love, one has to cultivate the power of unselfish love. The more a person gives in genuine love, the more he experiences an enlargement of being. His love returns a hundredfold. By the same token, the more he indulges in hatred, the more he experiences a contraction of being, a corrosion of the soul, a mutilation of personality. Hatred boomerangs as a self-destructive weapon. Apathy is also dangerously self-destructive, because it is most invidious. It kills the soul like a hidden cancer. That is why at the center of all the great religions of the world, love and compassion have been emphasized. God can truly be equated with love. In order to attain emotional maturity, passion has to evolve into compassion, and love has to be purged of its egotistical dross.

The development of man can never be adequate without the proper growth of his intellectual faculties. Reason is indeed a very distinctive endowment of man. It lifts him out of the immediacy of animal existence. It enables him to transform the chaotic flux of sense impressions into a cosmic order, into the meaningful environment in which he lives. It expands his mental horizon beyond the limitations of the present and affords him a glimpse of the eternal. The past, the present, and the future are revealed as inter-penetrative elements in the creative movement of the eternal. The present contains within it the entire past in a living and dynamic form. The future throbs in the heart of the present as hope and aspiration, as the self-transcending impulse, as the urge of self-overcoming.

Reason also liberates man from his animal status as a mere bundle of momentary impulses and instinctual drives. It gives them an upward orientation. It organizes them in the service of some great value or idea.

Intellectual development is essential for the conquest of confusion, disorder, and muddled thinking. Confused ideas can be responsible for a colossal waste of human effort and talent. Wrong ideas have misguided many honest souls. Without clear and consistent thinking, a person can be the victim of morbid sentimentalism. In the absence of proper intellectual training, religious faith degenerates into sectarianism, parochialism, fanaticism, ritualism, or occultism. One needs the sharp sword of a trained intellect to cut through the luxuriant growth of popular superstition.

But intellect has its limitations. Divorced from love and compassion, it may produce the apathetic attitude of aloofness. It may also produce much conceit and haughtiness, a sense of superiority, of towering above the teeming multitude. Intellectual conceit is a very invidious impediment to the full growth of personality.

By creating elaborate verbal and conceptual structures, intellect often prevents a direct encounter with reality. Too much reliance upon concepts and verbal symbols defeats man's ultimate purpose of comprehending reality. So while intellect is a great aid to development, it may also become a great obstacle to further progress. In order to capture a direct vision of the truth, one has to go beyond intellect. That is the abiding mission of all the great mystics of the world, eastern and western.

The development of man is also incomplete without the heightening of moral consciousness. Lopsided intellectual development often leads to the belief that the self of man is an epistemological subject—that man's highest goal lies in ivory-tower contemplation of reality away from the madding crowd. This is a grievous mistake. True wisdom is inseparable from active compassion and loving service. The spirit in man is no isolated consciousness. The human individual is inseparably a member of the social organism. His being is, as Martin Heidegger says, being-in-the-world.* So he cannot have complete fulfillment away from society and away from the world. Cultivation of solitude can only be a temporary resort for self-collectedness. To pursue solitude in the spirit of world- and life-negation is outrageous to one's integral being.

The human individual conceived of as a self-subsistent atom is a mere abstraction. Every individual grows through constant intercourse with his social environment. He draws upon the cultural heritage of society for his spiritual nourishment. He is expected to make a contribution of his own to the progress of society and culture.

There are different stages in the development of

* Martin Heidegger, *Being and Time* (New York: Harper and Row, 1962), p. 78*ff.*

moral consciousness. At the beginning morality assumes the form of respect for law and authority. It is such respect that distinguishes human society from the chaos of the jungle. The rule of law guarantees a certain measure of liberty to all members of the society. It saves man from utter insecurity in a state of anarchy. It also saves him from abject slavery under power-thirsty despotism.

Secondly, morality assumes the form of an inner vision of justice and righteousness in their purity. Such an inner vision is valid in proportion to the intensity and self-discipline of the individual.

The legal machinery of any existing society is certainly imperfect. There is room for improvement in all human institutions. Injustice is often done in the name of justice. Laws are often broken by the custodians of law themselves in order to suit their personal advantage. Hypocrisy is often practiced under the mask of social respectability. Rights of the social underdog are often mercilessly trampled underfoot by people in positions of power and authority. Glittering masks are worn to hide the ugly motives of greed and selfishness.

Morality in the second—and higher—form consists in the courageous lifting of one's voice against the lawless laws of the existing social order. It consists in taking a bold stand against legalized hypocrisy and accepting the dire consequences thereof. It consists in fighting for justice where injustice prevails; in fighting for truth where falsehood prevails; in fighting for legitimate rights where ruthless domination and exploitation prevail.

Thirdly, morality consists in a positive spirit of sharing with others. It implies a heightened sense of responsibility for all fellow beings. Such a sense of responsibility may stem from a keen perception of the close inter-relatedness of all life. What an individual does may directly or indirectly affect other individuals in the world. Moral consciousness therefore dictates a concern for others in all his actions. It inspires him on the path of dedication to the welfare of all.

The impulse to share with others may also be spiritually inspired by the vision of the One in the all of existence—by the realization of the indwelling presence of God in all living creatures. When this happens, moral behavior becomes a spontaneous outpouring of the spirit of cosmic love. One offers one's life in the service of the poor and the downtrodden; in feeding the hungry and clothing the naked; in healing the sick and sheltering the homeless. One does all this not because one has to, but because that is the great joy of one's life. One engages in such humanitarian services without any expectation of reward or recognition. Virtue is realized as its own reward. Moral consciousness reaches its highest fulfillment here.

The self-development of man cannot be complete without the awakening of the spirit in him. Authentic spiritual fulfillment is indeed the final phase of the balanced growth of personality.

Now, what is the meaning of the spirit? The spirit is the element of pure transcendence in man. It is that dimension of existence which is radically different from the physical, the intellectual, the emotional, and the moral aspects of personality. It transcends them all and yet pervades them and sustains them. It may be defined as the nontemporal dimension of existence. The ultimate goal of all higher religion and mysticism is man's self-awareness on this deepest level of personality.

What happens to an individual when he discovers the spiritual dimension of existence? He realizes his essential rootedness in the eternal. He is brought into the immediate presence of the Supreme. He finds himself alone with the Alone. He encounters that ineffable One in the medium of which all creatures live, move, and have their being. His perception of the world undergoes a profound transformation. He begins to see the world of space and time not as a self-subsistent process, but as a diversified expression of the eternal. He experiences the essential oneness of all existence in the identity of the Supreme Being.

Spiritual realization may be static or dynamic. In static spiritual realization, there is an orientation toward the transcendental aspect of the eternal. In consequence, the world appears as unreal or as incorrigibly evil. So contemplation is prized above action. Action is at best a means of self-purification preparatory to perfect contemplation. But in dynamic spiritual realization the eternal is experienced as the foundation of the creative movement of time. The world emerges into view as endowed with an intrinsic reality and significance of its own. It is the spacio-temporal and evolutionary medium of manifestation of the inexhaustible riches of the eternal. In consequence, action is perceived as of the very essence of human reality. It is no less real and valuable than contemplation. If action leads to contemplation, contemplation leads back to action. Realization of the eternal must issue forth into appropriate action in time —in selfless deeds of courage and love and good will to all fellow beings.

It is in dynamic self-realization that the physical, emotional, intellectual, and moral aspects of personality fall into their right places. Each functions as instrumental to the creative self-expression of the authentic self as an active center of the eternal. Lopsided development of any one of these aspects is ruled out as prejudicial to balanced living.

How do you attain dynamic spiritual fulfillment? An answer to this question has been attempted in my book *Integral Yoga*, and one brief word will suffice here. In striving for such fulfillment one has to be supported by two wings: dynamic self-offering to the eternal, and selfless action. Through different spiritual practices such as prayer, meditation, and self-inquiry, one has to surrender oneself more and more to the eternal as an egoless instrument thereof. Then one has to put into practice this attitude of self-surrender in daily living. Active regard for cosmic welfare is to be adopted as the ultimate criterion of all decisions. Various activities in life must be performed in the spirit of self-offering at the altar of collective good.

Total self-offering to the eternal produces genuine wisdom. Selfless action is of the essence of love. Wisdom perfects love as unmotivated self-giving in the service of the All. Love perfects wisdom as awareness of the oneness of all existence.

SOME QUEST BOOK TITLES

Man Visible and Invisible by C. W. Leadbeater

Thought-Forms by Annie Besant and C. W. Leadbeater

The Mystery of Healing edited by Adelaide Gardner

The Future is Now by Arthur W. Osborn

The Psychic Sense by Phoebe D. Payne and Laurence J. Bendit

The Etheric Double by A. E. Powell

Scientific Evidence of the Existence of the Soul by Benito F. Reyes

The Doctrine of the Subtle Body in Western Tradition by G. R. S. Mead

Meditation: A Practical Study by Adelaide Gardner

Concentration: An Approach to Meditation by Ernest Wood

Psychism and the Unconscious Mind, edited by H. Tudor Edmonds

For a complete list of all Quest Books write to:
QUEST BOOKS
P.O. Box 270, Wheaton, Ill. 60187